Achieving the SAT Breakthrough:
Acing the Types of Questions that Most Students Find Difficult

Focus On: Vocabulary

Published by Focus on Learning Publishing, LLC.®

Legal Notice

This book is copyright 2019 with all rights reserved. It is illegal to copy, distribute, or create derivative works from this book in whole or in part or to contribute to the copying, distribution, or creating of derivative works of this book.

Resources and Downloads:

www.folpbooks.com

This publication was written and edited by a combined team of teachers, writers, editors, and proofreaders at Focus on Learning Publishing, LLC. ® and Perfect Your Education ® test prep center.

Editor in Chief: Steve Martin

Authored by: Jan Park, Steve Martin, Jane Rapston, Minnie Shannon,

Editors: Jane Rapston, Stephanie Lewis

Contributors: Miles Crawford, Lenny Townsend, Jill Tau

Proofreaders: Peter Linnes, Melanie Williams, Sae Hee Choi

This product was developed by Focus on Learning Publishing, LLC.®

E-mail: info@focusonlearningpublishing.com
Website: www.folpbooks.com

SAT® is a registered trademark of the College Board, which is not affiliated with this publication.

Copyright © 2019 Focus on Learning Publishing, LLC.®
All rights reserved.

ISBN-13: 978-1-7330032-2-3

Focus On: Vocabulary

Table of Contents

1	The Abouts	iv
2	SAT® Tier 2 Vocabulary Explained, the Selection Process for this Book & How to Use this Book	v
3	Memorizing Vocabulary & the "Mesmerizing Memorization Method"	vi
4	How to Use the Test Questions Analysis Sheet	x
5	Test Questions Analysis Sheet - Reading Section	xi
12	Vocabulary Practice Questions	Pg 1
13	Answer Keys	Pg 98

The Abouts
About this book, the tests, and studying for the exam

About this Book & Other Books

This book is not meant to be a full-test prep book for the SAT® verbal and the math sections. This book is specifically for learning SAT® type Tier 2 vocabulary along with the assortment of questions to help learn, understand, and memorize these words. It is strongly suggested for you to get the full test prep books, or download tests from the internet, and then use this book and the other books in the Focus on: series of specific SAT® type questions to hone your ability on these questions. Focus on Learning Publishing LLC.® has teamed up with Perfect Your Education® test prep center to research the data on students' tests, analyze those tests and use the data from the results for which this series of SAT® test prep courses were created.

This book focuses on vocabulary. If you don't know a lot of vocabulary, now is the time to study. This book will teach you effective ways of memorizing vocabulary, along with exercises to fortify the memorization process.

For the word and definition pages, fill in the blank with the correct word from the unit's word box. Sometimes the word might need some structural changes made to it such as changing the verb from its base form to another tense. For example, the verb "play" is in its base form. If the sentence requires the verb to be changed into it past tense form "ed", you must make these changes in the blank. Structural changes that might need to be made include changing: verb tenses, the word form from a noun to an adjective, a verb to an adjective, and adjectives to adverbs.

Both exercise pages will require you to choose the correct definition being used and write those definitions on the lines provided. Think carefully about which word to use, determine which part of speech (grammar element) fits appropriately, and write the complete definition for best results.

About Practice Tests

By taking numerous SAT® practice exams, your ability to see patterns, learn the types of questions and get an in-depth feel of the exam will increase. Taking a practice test is only the beginning. Analyzing your practice tests and finding out which questions you need to improve on will be the fundamental work. After knowing the results of your analysis, you will be able to begin the real work of tackling the most wrongly answered questions, then going back to another practice test to begin the whole process all over again with different question types. Depending on how much time and effort you devote to your SAT® studies, the results will show through better scores.

About Studying for the Exam

There are many strategies, some in this book, which will help you to improve your score, but knowing the basics of the exam are important. The reading sections are comprised of literature, the humanities/social sciences, and physical sciences. The more that you read of these subjects, the better your chances of understanding them will be. Topics found in short stories, international short stories, popular literature, research papers, textbooks, such as slavery/abolition, women's suffrage, government, biology - human, animal, and plant- technology, and research studies are the kinds of articles you should read on a daily basis. Stories and books will be added to www.folpbooks.com for students to read. Knowing your grammar inside and out is key along with sentence and paragraph structures for the writing and language section. Lastly, learning the math concepts and practicing them through the processes of focused, diffused, and chunking- learning, relaxing, reabsorbing, practicing - then, starting all over for another topic and later coming back to the previous subjects again are key study methods that will help you with the math sections, and all sections.

Your score will be determined by how much planned effort you put into your studies, not just taking practice tests. You need to invest at least 30 min for the verbal and 30 for math daily for about one year to get great results, more than one year for outstanding results. In the case that you find SAT® type reading comprehension questions too difficult, Focus on Learning Publishing LLC. ® has come out with a book specifically for improving reading comprehension titled: <u>Focused On: Improving on Reading Comprehension for High School Students.</u> Again, as the saying goes, "Practice makes perfect." So, practice, practice, practice!

SAT Tier 2 Vocabulary Explained, the Selection Process for this Book & How to Use this Book

Tier 2 Words

The SAT® vocabulary questions are based on Tier 2 vocabulary words. Tier 2 vocabulary words are the work of educators Isabel L. Beck, Margaret G. McKeown, and Linda Kucan, who divided vocabulary into three tiers. Tier 1 being easy words that children would use such as desk, happy, and talk. Tier 2 words are words that we encounter daily, but are polysemous, meaning that these words can have multiple meanings across domains (Literature, science, mathematics, etc.). Tier 3 words are difficult level and subject-specific words. These include words such as obsequious, imperative, hyperbole.

Choosing the Words Based on Topics of Texts

The process that Focus on Learning Publishing, LLC. ® used to choose these tier 2 words was by reading numerous texts and using word-finding functions to locate the count of each word's instance in several texts about a subject. After concluding the process of determining which words to use, Focus on Learning Publishing, LLC. ® writers and editors wrote sentences, paragraphs, extracted excerpts from texts using the words to provide memorizing activities for students.

How to Use this Book

Memorizing vocabulary that have multiple meanings is what the SAT vocabulary questions are all about. This book is divided into units of five words with a total of 30 units amounting to one-hundred and fifty words in total. The activities in this book have been created based on teachers' experiences with students using passive memorization exercises. Exercises such as fill in the blanks using all of the multiple meanings of the words help the student see the difference in usage of the same word. By spacing the words among other words, it allows the student to differentiate the meanings of the words. Other exercises, such as finding the correct meaning of the word used in a sentence or a paragraph helps the student to know the meanings while memorizing them.

Each unit ends with a unit review made up of a word-definition match-up activity and a paragraph of fill in the blank sentences, mostly with the hardest words' and their little-known, inconspicuous, meanings.

Memorizing Vocabulary

Index Cards

The SAT® has a lot of easy words in the vocabulary type questions, or so that might seem. Though some easy words are found on the SAT®, the hard thing about them is that they might have multiple definitions, many which you may not know. This book was designed to give students ample practice with words and their multiple meanings, but using the tried-and-true memorization methods to commit these words to memory never hurts.

Almost everybody has used the index card memorization method to memorize vocabulary for tests. This method uses the 3" X 5" index cards as a visual aid to look at the word that is to be memorized, then look at the definition. The index card has one side which is all white. On this side of the card, you are to write the word in big letters, almost to fill up the entire space. The other side of the card has lines on it; these are for the definitions.

Begin the memorization process by looking at the word. Say it out loud, memorize its spelling, and see if you can find any word traits such as its prefix, base-word, and/or suffix. If you do, make a note of these traits to help with the memorization process. For example, if a word has the prefix "pro" in it, the word probably has a positive meaning because "pro" means "in favor of" or "forward" as in the word "progress", "to go forward". After looking at the word, flip the card over and look at its definition. Try to commit it to memory by saying it a few times out loud and then in your head. Continue doing this until you're pretty sure you have the word memorized then go onto the next word. Do this for a total of five words.

After memorizing five words, it's time for a little self-quiz. Go back to the first word and see if you remember it. If you do, put it at the bottom of the group of words. These will be your "memorized words". If you do not remember it, put it in a group of cards that you have separated from the known words. This group will be your "unmemorized words". Now that you've collected the words that you haven't fully memorized yet, go back and rememorize these words as you did with the others. Upon memorizing the unmemorized group, put them back with the original five, then resume memorizing a new set of five words. At the bottom of this new set, put the previous five so that when you get to them again, you can see if you have fully committed these words to memory, as well as the new set of words.

This process should be ongoing and repeated until all the words in this book, and any other vocabulary lists, are all memorized. View the pictures of the cards below as examples of how to make your own.

Define

1. To define the meaning of a word, phrase, symbol, sign, etc.
2. To describe, explain, or make definite and clear.
3. To demark sharply the outlines or limits of an area or concept.
4. To determine with precision; to mark out with distinctness.

Writing Your Own Sentences

Another technique for memorizing words with multiple meanings is to write your own sentences using the definitions provided at the beginning of each unit.

The word being used for this example is "**sector**". The word sector has 5 definitions:

1. (n.) section, a part
2. (n.) zone (designated area controlled by military).
3. (n.) part of a circle, extending to the center
4. (n.) a field of economic activity
5. (n.) an instrument consisting of two rulers of equal length joined by a hinge used for solving problems in proportion, trigonometry, multiplication and division, and for various functions, such as squares and cube roots.

Based on those 5 definitions, make 5 of your own sentences. Below are 5 sentences in numerical order with the above definitions.

Def 1 When a **sector** of the Kaloko Dam broke in 1892, the flood cost many lives and millions in damage.

Def 2 After the second world war, Berlin was divided into four different **sectors**.

Def 3 These lines divide the circle into four equal **sectors**.

Def 4 Public **sector** jobs include professions from firefighters and the police through to civil servants.

Def 5 A **sector** can be made from two sticks and a hinge for usage carpentry, astrology, and more.

Write & Record

Rote memorization through writing is one of the oldest memorization techniques. By writing the words and their multiple definitions down on paper, say ten times, you are not just seeing them, you are actively memorizing them through the act of writing. An additional technique is taking those written words and recording them onto a device such as a cell phone or a tablet, then listening to them played back. By doing this, you are using not just one facet of your brain, but multiple senses, touch, sight, and hearing. By using more than one sense, you are connecting these senses on one purpose: memorizing words, and the effect can be greater than just viewing the words and definitions as in the index card method alone.

Mesmerizing Memorization Method

This method brings vocabulary memorization, or any kind of memorization, to a whole new level. In the "Mesmerizing Memorization Method", you will do most of the memorizing with your eyes closed and picturing the words and definitions in your mind. This method, coupled with the previous methods of using your other senses will prove to be very helpful. By implementing all of these methods, especially the "Mesmerizing Memorization Method", a few of the committed and diligent, Perfect Your Education test prep center's students were able to memorize and retain 100 words per day. However, this amount was not the average amount memorized. Most students were comfortable memorizing 25 words a day.

Since you'll be doing most of this memorization technique in your head, you need a quiet, calm, and comfortable place to do it. Close your eyes and imagine that you are in the center of a theater. You should be center from the front and back as well as the left and right walls of the theater. You will be the only person in the whole theater; all of the other chairs should be empty. Look up at the white screen where the movie would normally be projected on and visualize your first word. Imagine its correct spelling at the center of the white screen. Visualize and say the word internally for about five seconds. Then have that word fade out and have the word's first definition replace it on the screen. Visualize and repeat the definition about ten times. Go back and forth between the word and definition about ten to twenty times. The final step is to put them both together by visualizing the word on the top half of the screen and the definition on the bottom half. After completing this first definition, go back and do the same steps for the second, third, or however many definitions the word has for it. After completing this, you'll pretty much have that word memorized after concluding these steps. Continue the same steps for all words and definitions in that unit.

Upon completing all the words and definitions in a unit, you should test yourself to see if you have committed them to memory. However, before memorizing the words, set aside a paper with all of the words prewritten, but not the definitions, only the words with numbering (1., 2.,3., etc.) After you complete all of the steps for "Mesmerizing Memorization Method", put all of the vocabulary away except for that one sheet, then test yourself. Whichever words you get wrong on the self-test, restart the "Mesmerizing Memorization Method" for those words only. Upon memorizing those words, take a break before going on to another unit of words. By doing this, students have memorized up to 100 words a day and could possibly do even more!

Other strategies for figuring out words' definitions

Though knowing your vocabulary is the surest way to improve on SAT® vocabulary-based questions, there are some other ways for you to know what a word means. Using context clues allows for you to know the general meaning of a word. Look at the other words in the sentence and figure out what the word in question means. For example, in the following sentence, "The deceptive liar was disliked by most of her classmates resulting from their distrust of her." If the person did not know the word deceptive, they would most likely be able to tell from the words "liar", "disliked", and "distrust" that the word deceptive has a negative meaning. By using the words near the unknown word, we can somewhat know what the meaning of the word is, then guess from the answer choices that are similar to that unknown word's meaning.

Understanding the Phrases, Expressions, Idioms, and Subject Specific Terms

After you memorize the vocabulary, you need to understand the colloquial (conversational style language), literary, archaic (language of the past), and subject-specific/technical phrases, idioms, as well as lingo used in most writing. Read texts on slavery, women's suffrage, biology, technology, science in general, literature from the past, social issues, the humanities. The language used just over one-hundred years ago and now are quite different from each other, so it is important to familiarize yourself with these kinds of texts. Many of these texts can be found at www.folpbooks.com free to read. By memorizing and doing exercises in these books, your understanding of elements that make up sentences will improve. This is not something that you can do overnight. To continue this work on improving your ability to understand words for the SAT® examination, you should read daily. Not only can you find such texts as described at www.folpbooks.com, but numerous internet websites also have nearly any article about every subject. If you focus on reading the topics on the SAT® exam— those being literature, social sciences and humanities, and the physical sciences, along with writing down and memorizing words from these texts— you will increase your chances of greatly improving your reading ability and subsequently your score. A list of the specific types of SAT® passages can be found at www.folpbooks.com. Months of practice and memorization come into play for memorizing and comprehending these elements of sentences, so you should give yourself at least a year of study before you take the actual SAT®.

Summer is the best time to study for the SAT® especially in your sophomore and junior years since a new SAT® date has been added for August. This means that you can focus on increasing your SAT® score during the whole summer without the interruption of other tests, projects, school responsibilities. You can focus a large amount of the summer vacation on SAT® studies. So, if you did not achieve your desired score, plan on taking the SAT® early in your senior year.

How to Use the Test Questions Analysis Sheet:

The purpose of the Test Questions Analysis Sheet is to find out and record which questions on the practice tests you answered incorrectly so that you know which types of questions you need to improve on to increase your score. Each box has a specific type of question from the exam in which you will write your incorrectly answered questions. The steps to determine what you incorrectly answered are as follows:

Take a practice test, available for free online, then check the test with its answer key to determine which questions you got wrong. In the box with that type of question on the Test Questions Analysis Sheet, write the number of the question you got wrong. When you finish the entire test, you should have the boxes filled with the numbers. The boxes with the most questions wrong in them will tell you what types of questions you need to work on to improve. Count up the amount of wrongly answered questions and write that number next to the type of question at the top of each column, or in the notes section of the page. Those numbers will tell you how many you answered incorrectly for that type of question. Based on those numbers, you can purchase whichever of Focus on Learning Publishing LLC.® Focus On: series specifically made for those types of questions. You may need to take multiple tests to gather enough data on what you got wrong. It is best to get data from at least three tests to determine which questions students got wrong. However, to jump right in to studying, one test will be enough to see which questions were answered incorrectly.

Many students incorrectly answered the vocabulary questions third most often than other questions because they did not know the various definitions besides the commonly known ones. Based on this data, we made this Focus On: series of question-specific courses. On the following page, you will find the Test Questions Analysis Sheet.

You should copy the Test Questions Analysis Sheet and use it on all of the passages in this book.

Focus On: Vocabulary

Test Questions Analysis Sheet - Reading Section

	Detail / Fact	Inference	Word-in-Context / Vocab	Big Idea	Small idea
T-1					
T-2					
T-3					
T-4					
T-5					
	Author's Meaning / interpretation	Author's Purpose / Specific purpose	Author's / Passage Tone	Data Analysis- Graphic/chart	Line Reference
T-1					
T-2					
T-3					
T-4					
T-5					
	Function	Dual passage Comparison	Dual passage Author's POV	Notes:	
T-1					
T-2					
T-3					
T-4					
T-5					

*for a complete meaning of each type of question, go to www.folpbooks.com

Vocabulary Practice Questions

Focus On: Vocabulary

Unit 1:
Advocate - Industrious - Fundamental - Definition - Consequent

A) Know the definitions - Read through each definition and get a feeling for the meaning of each. If you choose to, memorize the words as explained in "Mesmerizing Memorization Method".

Advocate

(n.) Someone whose job is to speak for someone's case in a court of law.
(n.) A person who speaks in support of something.
(v.) To plead in favor of; to defend by argument, before a tribunal or the public; to support.
(v.) To encourage support for something.

Industrious

(adj.) Hard-working and persistent.

Fundamental

(n.) A primary principle, rule, or law, which serves as the groundwork of a system; an essential part.
(adj.) Pertaining to the foundation or basis; serving for the foundation.
(adj.) Essential, as an element, principle, or law; important; original; elementary.

Definition

(n.) A statement of the meaning of a word or word group or a sign or symbol.
(n.) The action or power of describing, explaining, or making definite and clear.
(n.) Clarity of visual presentation, distinctness of outline or detail.
(n.) Clarity, especially of musical sound in reproduction.
(n.) Sharp demarcation (showing the limits) of outlines or limits.
(n.) The degree to which individual muscles are distinct on the body.

Consequent

(n.) Following as a result, inference, or natural effect.
(n.) An event which follows another.

Focus On: Vocabulary

B) Fill in the blanks with the correct word from this unit's words, make necessary structural changes to the word, then write the correct definition of the word being used on the line below the sentence.

1) Animal activists _____ the fair treatment of all animals.
_____

2) By _____, playing means having fun and not working or studying.
_____

3) The _____ walked the plaintiff through all the steps needed to be done.
_____

4) People's _____ of personal circumstances are often different from others.
_____

5) When a student acts inappropriately in class, the _____ is usually a punishment.
_____

6) This sound system has superior _____ to all the other competition.
_____

7) The _____ ideas for our type of government came from ancient Greece's democracy.
_____

8) My daughter was very _____ while learning to ride the unicycle for her school's circus.
_____

9) As we can see, the _____ of the individual cells are marked by their walls.
_____

10) His retirement and _____ spare time enabled him to travel more.
_____

11) That weight-lifter swears that _____ is more important than bulk.
_____

12) Most people would agree that a(n) _____ aspect of learning is studying.
_____

13) Susan B. Anthony is remembered as a great _____ for the suffrage movement.
_____

14) One of the _____ of linear algebra is matrices.
_____

15) The congressman _____ for a national debt forgiveness program for debtors.
_____

16) I couldn't believe the _____ of the tremendous TV in his entertainment room.
_____

C) Choose the correct definition from the word list page, then write it under the given paragraphs.

1) I am not touching in this picture merely to attack it. It has been abundantly attacked; what it needs is **definition**. For there is much in this bourgeois, good-humored American literature of ours which rings true, which is as honest an expression of our individuality as was the more austere product of antebellum New England. If American sentimentality does invite criticism, American sentiment deserves defense.

_____

_____

_____

2) All across the US, students attend school with very few of them really knowing the stakes at hand. These few short years of high school are the years that can either propel some on a path to quick success, or a chaotic labyrinth to many dead ends. Those students wise and **industrious** enough to study what the "real world" needs – primarily math, science, and computer-related subjects- will find that their futures will be fulfilling, as well as secure.

_____

_____

_____

3) All this must not be taken in too absolute a sense. There are medicines, and good ones, in the hands of writers and of critics, to abate, if not to heal, this plague of sentimentalism. I have stated ultimate causes only. They are enough to keep the mass of Americans reading sentimentalized fiction until some **fundamental** change has come, not strong enough to hold back the van of American writing, which is steadily moving toward restraint, sanity, and truth. Every honest composition is a step forward in the cause; and every clear-minded criticism.

_____

_____

_____

4) She still suffered from backache and general languor, **consequent** upon over-rapid growth during the year she had spent on the flat of her back. Old Nurse pitied and was much inclined to spoil her, dosed her religiously with a glass of port at eleven o'clock every morning, and supported her whining assertions that lessons with Mademoiselle made her ill. Still, being so young, an education is what she needed, and an education is what she would get.

_____

_____

_____

5) In the general concern for the Superior-General's, Mother Gertrude, welfare and admiration of her courage in undertaking such a journey on the eve of her sixty-third birthday, it seemed to Alex that all other considerations were overlooked or ignored entirely. She was aware that the convent spirit of detachment (not showing of emotions), so much **advocated**, and the consciousness of that vow of obedience made freely and fully, would alike preclude the possibility of any spoken protest or lamentation over the separation.

_____

_____

_____

Unit 2:
Commodity - Authority - Major - Individual - Complacent

A) Know the definitions - Read through each definition and get a feeling for the meaning of each. If you choose to, memorize the words as explained in "Mesmerizing Memorization Method".

Commodity

(n.) Any movable good that is bought and sold; An essential good from agriculture, raw materials, etc.
(n.) Something useful or valuable.

Authority

(n.) The power to enforce rules or give orders.
(n.) Persons in command; specifically, government.
(n.) A person accepted as a source of reliable information on a subject.
(n.) Government-owned agency which runs a revenue-generating activity.

Major

(n.) Title for an army officer with the rank of major.
(n.) A field of specialized academic study.
(adj.) Of great significance or importance.
(adj.) Having significance in size or amount; a great amount.
(v.) To study an academic field as the main study.

Individual

(n.) A person considered alone, rather than as belonging to a group of people.
(n.) One part belonging to a population or group.
(adj.) Relating to a single person or thing as opposed to more than one.

Complacent

(adj.) Uncritically satisfied with oneself or one's achievements; smug.
(adj.) Not caring with regard to an apparent need or problem.

Focus On: Vocabulary

B) Fill in the blanks with the correct word from the word list, make necessary structural changes to the word, then write the correct definition of the word being used on the line below the sentence.

1) Unwrap each _____ cheese slice and put it on the bread.
_____

2) The new recruits saluted the _____ when he entered the barracks.
_____

3) Most people who enter Manhattan by bus enter it at the New York Port _____.
_____

4) Although courage, resolve, and tenacity are important _____, moral conduct trumps all.
_____

5) The hikers said they saw a suspicious _____ coming out of a cave near here.
_____

6) The world's foremost _____ on aliens is entering the spaceship now.
_____

7) The US is a(n) _____ player in international politics.
_____

8) As people become more self-centered, they also become _____ with people's problems.
_____

9) The Supreme Court of the United States is the ultimate _____ on the Constitution.
_____

10) The runner was _____ about any race in his final years.
_____

11) Our son is _____ in mechanical engineering at a large university.
_____

12) Any _____ who wants extra credit should stay after class.
_____

13) The student's _____ is geology.
_____

14) He lost all his _____ and respect after yelling hysterically at the meeting.
_____

15) Tradable _____ are categorized into four groups: agriculture, livestock, energy, and metals.
_____

16) The entire sanctuary needed a(n) _____ overhaul due to its outdated look.
_____

C) Choose the correct definition from the word list page, then write it under the given paragraphs.

1) **Complacent** people are the same drag on a society that a brake would be to a car going uphill. They are the "eternal negative" and would extinguish, if they could, any light stronger than that to which their weak eyes have been accustomed. They look with astonishment and distrust at anyone trying to break away from their tiresome old ways and habits, and wonder why all the world is not as pleased with their personalities as they are themselves. No blight, no mildew is more fatal to a plant than the "complacent" are to the world.

_____

_____

_____

2) There is nothing in the peculiar nature or uses of the precious metals which should make them an exception to the general principles of demand. So far as they are wanted for purposes of luxury or the arts, the demand increases with the cheapness, in the same irregular way as the demand for any other **commodity**. So far as they are required for money, the demand increases with the cheapness in a perfectly regular way, the quantity needed being always in inverse proportion to the value. This is the only real difference, with respect to demand, between money and other things.

_____

_____

_____

3) For the highest and deepest pleasure of civilized and cultivated man a combination of the best physical and mental emotions—with a little disappointment and grief—is essential; one without the other is always unsatisfying. Here, foremost among the mental experiences, so powerful as to have a certain physical influence, is our hope. The **major** force of all life is hope. It is life itself, for without it the scheme of human existence would collapse. To look forward, to anticipate, to hope for better things, and believe in them—that is the principle of life.

_____

_____

_____

4) I had a discussion recently with a Briton on the pronunciation of a word. As there is no "Institute," as in France, to settle matters of this kind, I maintained that we Americans had as much **authority** for our pronunciation of this particular word as the English. The answer was characteristic of arrogance: "I know I am right," said my Island friend, "because that is the way I pronounce it!"

_____

_____

_____

5) The middle-aged businessman golfer is an important **individual** in the general golfing scheme of things in the United States. Well enough does he know how the game is good for him. The early American golfers adopted the game in regard to creating and preserving physical fitness. The American businessman leads a quick life and a hard one and, in recent years particularly, his pursuit of this physical fitness has become something of a craze with him.

_____

_____

_____

Unit 3:
Approach - Section - Unprecedented - Formula - Document

A) Know the definitions - Read through each definition and get a feeling for the meaning of each. If you choose to, memorize the words as explained in "Mesmerizing Memorization Method".

Approach

(v.) To come or go near, in place or time.
(v.) To come near to a character or value.
(v.) To make an attempt at, as in solving a problem or making a policy.
(v.) To speak to, as to make a request or ask a question.
(n.) The way an aircraft comes on to land at an airport.

Section

(n.) A part, piece, subdivision of anything.
(v.) To cut, divide, or separate into pieces.

Unprecedented

(adj.) Never before seen, done, or experienced.

Formula

(n.) Any mathematical rule expressed symbolically.
(n.) A symbolic expression of the structure of a chemical compound.
(n.) A plan or method for dealing with a problem or for achieving a result.
(n.) A mixture or solution made in a prescribed manner.

Document

(n.) An original or official paper used as the basis, proof, or support of anything else.
(n.) A file that contains text, or numbers.
(v.) To record in documents.
(v.) To furnish with documents or papers necessary to establish facts or give information.

Focus On: Vocabulary

B) Fill in the blanks with the correct word from the word list, make necessary structural changes to the word, then write the correct definition of the word being used on the line below the sentence.

1) H_2O is the _____ for water.
_____

2) The hysterical woman _____ the police officer in search of her children.
_____

3) An automobile should be _____ according to the directions of law.
_____

4) The student _____ the extremely difficult equation in a way that astonished all.
_____

5) I've forgotten the _____ for finding the roots of a quadratic equation.
_____

6) The scientist_____ each step of the experiment.
_____

7) My son is _____ the age of manhood.
_____

8) The company's _____ for success includes excellent service and cheap prices.
_____

9) As autumn _____, we needed to prepare the crops for harvesting.
_____

10) The _____ for gunpowder was unknown in Europe until the 13th century.
_____

11) _____ and testimonies are important for a court case.
_____

12) We are witnessing a(n) _____ increase in bossiness being accepted as a norm in society.
_____

13) Security agents _____ off the area of the President's location.
_____

14) The Cessna C172 light aircraft has a(n) _____ speed of 65 knots.
_____

15) The _____ carried the seal of the governor's office.
_____

16) A broad _____ of the population now recognizes the need for political change.
_____

Focus On: Vocabulary

C) Choose the correct definition from the word list page, then write it under the given paragraphs.

1) The application of a drop of a strong solution of platinum tetrachloride to the rod will, on drying, give rise to a film of the dry salt, and this may be reduced in the luminous gas flame. During the process, however, the quartz is apt to get rotten, especially if the temperature has been anything **approaching** a full red heat. The resulting platinum deposit adheres very strongly to the quartz and may be soldered to as before. This method has been employed by the writer with success since 1887, and may even be extended to thick threads.

_____

_____

_____

2) In addition to oxygen and nitrogen at least two other substances, namely, carbon dioxide and water vapor, must be present in the atmosphere in order that life may exist. The former of these is a gaseous compound of carbon and oxygen having the **formula** CO_2. Its presence in the air may be shown by causing the air to bubble through a solution of calcium hydroxide ($Ca(OH)_2$), commonly called lime water.

_____

_____

_____

3) Although accustomed to **unprecedented** deeds on your part, our hopes have been surpassed by your victory at the battle of Bassano. What glory is yours, immortal Bonaparte! Moreau was about to effect a juncture with you when that wretched retreat of Jourdan upset all our plans. Do not forget that immediately, the armies go into winter quarters on the Rhine; the Austrians will have forces available to help prepare camp.

_____

_____

_____

4) The Abolitionists, after this insult, determined to withdraw from the hearing and appeal to the legislature to be heard, not as a favor but of right. A new hearing was therefore ordered and the reformers appeared a second time before the committee. But the scenes of the first were repeated at the second hearing. The chairman was intolerably insolent to the speakers. His violent behavior to William Goodell, who was paying his respects to the Southern **documents** lying on the table of the committee, terminated the second hearing.

_____

_____

_____

5) Montgomery is favorably located for being one of the largest lumber marts in the South, owing to her close proximity to the immense body of longleaf pine in South Alabama. On all the rivers and streams in this **section** abound hardwoods of every kind, suitable for manufacture into furniture, wagons, tool handles and for every variety of woodworking.

_____

_____

_____

Unit 4:
Concept - Significant - Process - Utilize - Scrupulous

A) Know the definitions - Read through each definition and get a feeling for the meaning of each. If you choose to, memorize the words as explained in "Mesmerizing Memorization Method".

Concept

(n.) Abstract and general idea.
(n.) Understanding retained in the mind, from experience, reasoning and/or imagination.

Significant

(adj.) Carrying meaning.
(adj.) Having a noticeable or major effect; having importance.
(adj.) Reasonably large in number or amount.

Process

(n.) A series of events which produce a result.
(n.) A set of procedures used to produce a product.
(n.) A task or program executed on a computer.
(v.) To perform a particular process on a thing.
(v.) To think about a piece of information, or a concept, in order to take it in, and perhaps accept it.

Utilize

(v.) To make useful; to find a practical use for.
(v.) To make best use of; to use to its fullest extent, potential, or ability.
(v.) To use in a manner different from that originally intended.

Scruple (Scrupulous)

(adj.) Exactly and carefully done.
(n.) Hesitation to act from the difficulty of determining what is right or expedient.
(v.) To hesitate or be reluctant to act due to considerations of conscience.

Focus On: Vocabulary

B) Fill in the blanks with the correct word from this unit's words, make necessary structural changes to the word, then write the correct definition of the word being used on the line below the sentence.

1) The _____ taught at the workshop will help us to change our way of thinking.
_____

2) Responsibility is a(n) _____ word to most people.
_____

3) The sketchy lady wouldn't _____ to lie if she thought it would help her.
_____

4) The cook will _____ the leftover lamb bones to make a soup.
_____

5) All of the _____ needed to be done by the computer will take some time.
_____

6) The _____ of making a chair from scratch is time consuming.
_____

7) That conman is without _____.
_____

8) _____ the drones to plant seeds at a faster rate than by hand.
_____

9) Photosynthesis is the _____ in which oxygen is produced by plants.
_____

10) We must consider how best to _____ what resources we have.
_____

11) The butcher _____ the entire cow without wasting a single part of it.
_____

12) He has a(n) _____ amount of money.
_____

13) People should have a clear _____ of what freedom is.
_____

14) I will need some time to _____ all of this new information about the subject.
_____

15) Since he is an accountant, he is _____ in his finances.
_____

16) The CEO's new plan was a(n) _____ step for the company's future.
_____

C) Choose the correct definition from the word list page, then write it under the given paragraphs.

1) In addition to the contradictions and complications of science already mentioned, scarcely a fundamental principle or **concept** remains. One of the eternal indisputable postulates of science was that "two bodies cannot occupy the same space at the same time." But that is exploded, and we know they do, and we have proof of it every day. There are numerous instances; I will mention only one: Twenty-eight electric currents can pass over the same wire at the same time, fourteen one way and fourteen the other, and occupy the same space and do not interfere with one another.

_____

_____

_____

2) During the course of the year of 1945, the President directed the seizure of many of the nation's industries in the course of labor disputes. The total number of facilities taken over is **significant**: two railroad systems, one public utility, nine industrial companies, the transportation systems of two cities, the motor carriers in one city, a towing company and a butadiene plant. In addition thereto, the President on April 10 seized 218 bituminous coal mines belonging to 162 companies and on May 7, 33 more bituminous mines of 24 additional companies.

_____

_____

_____

3) Good poetry seizes the moment, the situation, the thought; drags it palpitating from life and flings it, quivering with its own rhythmic movement, into expression. The thing cannot be done in mere prose, for there is more than explanation to the **process**. The words themselves, in their color and suggestiveness, the rhythms that carry them, contribute to the sense, even as overtones help to make the music.

_____

_____

_____

4) The utmost care was bestowed upon the training and education of the children. There was nothing that I met with in that beautiful and happy country I longed more to bring with me to the inhabitants of my world, than their manner of rearing children. The most **scrupulous** attention was paid to their diet and exercise, both mental and physical. The result was plump limbs, healthy, happy faces, and joyous spirits.

_____

_____

_____

5) Animals and domestic fowls had long been extinct in Mizora. This was one cause of the weird silence that so impressed me on my first view of their capital city. Invention had superseded the usefulness of animals in all departments: in the field and the chemistry of food. Artificial power was **utilized** for all vehicles. This power was created by using several highly technological techniques which further alienated all life.

_____

_____

_____

Unit 5:
Resource - Acquire - Feature - Strategy - Ensure

A) Know the definitions - Read through each definition and get a feeling for the meaning of each. If you choose to, memorize the words as explained in "Mesmerizing Memorization Method".

Resource

(n.) Something that is used to achieve an objective, e.g. raw materials or personnel.
(n.) A person's capacity to deal with a situation.
(v.) To supply with resources.

Acquire

(v.) To gain, usually by one's own efforts.
(v.) To contract.

Feature

(n.) An important or main item.
(n.) A long, prominent article or item in the media.
(n.) Any of the physical constituents of the face, such as eyes, nose, etc.
(n.) A beneficial capability of a piece of software.
(n.) Characteristic forms or shapes of parts. e.g. a hole, boss, slot, cut, chamfer, or fillet.
(v.) To state or show that something is the greatest importance to another thing within a certain context.
(v.) To appear; to make an appearance.

Strategy

(n.) The science and art of military command for overall planning and conduct of warfare.
(n.) A plan of action intended to accomplish a specific goal.
(n.) The art of using devised techniques in politics or business.

Ensure

(v.) To make sure or certain of something.
(v.) To make a pledge to (someone); to promise, guarantee.

Focus On: Vocabulary

B) Fill in the blanks with the correct word from this unit's words, make necessary structural changes to the word, then write the correct definition of the word being used on the line below the sentence.

1. The mouse pointer is the best _____ of a computer's operating system.
   _____

2. The parents' _____ for the rebellious child produced a positive result.
   _____

3. All children receive a public education, for the most part, _____ by the state.
   _____

4. In the past, many children _____ horrible deadly diseases.
   _____

5. Freedom is a key _____ of our society.
   _____

6. After Skip moved out of his parents' house, he had to rely on his own _____ to live.
   _____

7. This month our magazine will publish a special _____ on the President.
   _____

8. All of the company's _____ were pulled together to solve the problem.
   _____

9. The archeologist _____ "Lucy" as the prime example of a pre-human hominid.
   _____

10. Much planning prevails over little _____, so those with no tactics lose.
    _____

11. My favorite band has never before _____ in the top ten.
    _____

12. Both Napoleon's and Hitler's _____ against Russia cost them their wars.
    _____

13. I use an alarm clock to _____ that I get up on time.
    _____

14. These tiny holes are a new _____ which makes this engine perform better.
    _____

15. I will _____ that the car arrives by six o'clock.
    _____

16. He _____ a noble title.
    _____

17. His piercing blue eyes were his best _____.
    _____

C) Choose the correct definition from the word list page, then write it under the given paragraphs.

1) Improving the futures of children in the care of the state, assisting the hard-to-reach families, and providing educational excellence should be some of the goals of government, but just saying so does not substantiate such goals. If we as a nation are seriously committed to improving opportunities for all, those goals must be supported and **resourced**. Government cuts to tax credits and universal credit, the disastrous cuts in support for those with disabilities, closing down public and private agencies ending the education funds make the attainment of those goals much more difficult.

_____

_____

_____

2) Now a definite course of study is very hard to construct,—a course that will tell exactly what the pupils of each grade should **acquire** each term or half-term in the way of habits, knowledge, ideals, attitudes, and prejudices. But such a course of study is the first requisite to efficiency in teaching. The system that goes by hit or miss, letting each teacher work out his own salvation in any way that he may see fit, is just a plan for failure.

_____

_____

_____

3) When the ice takes in early November, the caribou make it their great rallying ground. These animals, so wary in summer and early autumn, appear to gain confidence by their numbers, and are easily stalked and all too easily hunted. It is to be feared that too great an annual toll is taken, and that the herd is being diminished by more than the amount of its natural increase. More stringent regulations, the allowance of one caribou, instead of two, the forbidding of shooting in December and January, when the bulls have lost their horns, would affect the result and would **ensure** excellent sport in the region for a long time to come.

_____

_____

_____

4) Another important step emphasized by the recent writers is the need for training children to pick out the significant **features** in the text or portion of the text that they are reading. This, of course, is work that is to be undertaken from the very moment that they begin to use books. Knowing how to do it will amply repay study and experimentation by the individual teacher.

_____

_____

_____

5) Another shorter and less empirical way must be found to acquire the understanding of chess play. My system of teaching differs from the usual ones, in that it sets down at the outset definite elementary principles of chess **strategy** by which any move can be gauged at its true value, thus enabling the learner to form his own judgment as to the maneuvers under consideration. In my opinion, it is absolutely essential to follow such strategic principles for the development and conduct of a correct game of chess.

_____

_____

_____

Unit 1-5 Review

Match the correct definition with the correct word by writing the correct definition' letter in the blank next to the word that corresponds to that definition.

_____1. Feature

_____2. Commodity

_____3. Complacent

_____4. Process

_____5. Fundamental

_____6. Approach

_____7. Resource

_____8. Advocate

_____9. Unprecedented

_____10. Scrupulous

A. To make an attempt at as in solving a problem

B. To state or show that something is the greatest importance to another thing within a certain context

C. To plead in favor of

D. Never before seen, done, or experienced

E. To think about a piece of information

F. Something that is used to achieve an objective

G. Not caring with regard to an apparent need or problem

H. Pertaining to the foundation or basis;

I. Exactly and carefully done

J. An essential good from agriculture, raw materials

Fill in the blanks with the correct word from this unit's words:

While it is important that elementary school teachers teach math, language arts, science, and other subjects, their primary focus should be on helping students build up _____ work and study habits for their future educational career. Well-_____ research suggests that this is best done through as much one-on-one instruction with the teacher as possible. A competent teacher will know how to balance teaching an entire classroom while _____ his or her students get the _____ attention they need as well. This is a _____; every teacher must take the time to find what works best between themselves and their students.

Unit 6:
Role - Variable - Security - Equate - Taut

A) Know the definitions - Read through each definition and get a feeling for the meaning of each. If you choose to, memorize the words as explained in "Mesmerizing Memorization Method".

Role

(n.) A character or part played by a performer or actor.
(n.) The expected behavior of an individual in a society.
(n.) The function or position of something.

Variable

(adj.) Able to vary or change.
(adj.) Marked by diversity or difference.
(adj.) Having no fixed quantitative value.
(n.) A quantity that may assume any one of a set of values.

Security

(n.) The condition of not being threatened, esp. physically, psychologically, emotionally, or financially.
(n.) Something that secures the fulfillment of an obligation or law.
(n.) A tradable financial asset, such as a share of stock.
(n.) A guarantee.

Equate

(v.) To consider equal or equivalent.

Taut

(adj.) Tight; under tension, as it were a rope or bowstring.
(adj.) Extremely tense, or experiencing stress or anxiety.
(adj.) Containing only relevant parts, brief and controlled.

Focus On: Vocabulary

B) Fill in the blanks with the correct word from this unit's words, make necessary structural changes to the word, then write the correct definition of the word being used on the line below the sentence.

1) This legally binding document will provide the _____ for our business collaboration.
_____

2) The teacher praised the student for her _____ story; only the pertinent details were in it.
_____

3) Local volunteers played an important _____ in cleaning the beach after the oil spill.
_____

4) Depending on the _____ expenses of a month, my account may or may not have funds.
_____

5) His friends who lent him money did so on no _____ but his bare word.
_____

6) The _____ of women has changed significantly in the last decade.
_____

7) The gated community provides _____ for those people.
_____

8) Be careful going out, _____ high winds are predicted for this weekend.
_____

9) You cannot _____ acing an examination with being intelligent.
_____

10) The equity _____, also known as common stocks, are what traders trade on Wall Street.
_____

11) My neighbor was the lead _____ in last year's village play.
_____

12) His outward appearance was calm, but inside he was very _____.
_____

13) We must review several pricing _____ before setting the final price.
_____

14) The young boy could not pull back the _____ bowstring.
_____

15) The potassium content of food is very _____.
_____

Focus On: Vocabulary

C) Choose the correct definition from the word list page, then write it under the given paragraphs.

1) In Spain and Portugal, Freemasonry has played not merely a subversive but an actively revolutionary and sanguinary **role**. The anarchist Ferrer, intimately concerned with a plot to murder the King of Spain, was at the same moment entrusted with negotiations between the Grand Orient of France and the Grand Lodge of Catalonia. These murderous schemers, frustrated in Spain, met, however, in Portugal with complete success. The Portuguese revolutions from 1910 to 1921 were organized under the direction of Freemasonry and the Carbonarios.

_____
_____
_____

2) The size which any **variable** organ can reach does not appear to be governed by any principle of correlation. Large flowers are not necessarily accompanied by large leaves. The general tendency of a plant varying freely under artificial conditions seems to be atavistic—or to shed adaptive modifications which have ceased to be useful, and to revert to a more generalized type, or to reproduce characters which are already present in other members of the same group.

_____
_____
_____

3) Then one day they came close to the hedge, and suddenly they turned to us. They turned in a whirl and the movement of their body stopped as if slashed off, as suddenly as it had started. They stood still as a stone, and they looked straight upon us, straight into our eyes. There was no smile on their face, and no welcome. But their faces were **taut**, and their eyes were dark. Then they turned as swiftly, and they walked away.

_____
_____
_____

4) To help enter a state of hypnosis, I often use music. The first musical selection is Brahms' "Lullaby." Children's music boxes invariably contain this selection, and the melody cannot help but activate a pleasant nostalgia. It is a memory associated with love and tenderness. This brings us to the fact that hypnosis may offer the subject a chance to escape from the reality of pressing problems into a state of complete irresponsibility. In fact, one theory of hypnosis **equates** the hypnotic state as a form of unconscious regression and need for submission.

_____
_____
_____

5) There is no doubt whatsoever, that sanctuaries ought to be established, no matter how well the laws are enforced over both leaseholds and open areas. Civilized man is appreciating them more and more every day; and every day he is becoming better able to reach them. By giving absolute **security** to all desirable species in at least two different localities we can keep objects of Nature study in the best possible way both for ourselves and our posterity.

_____
_____
_____

Unit 7:
Eccentric - Interpret - Doctrine - Circumstance - Framework

A) Know the definitions - Read through each definition and get a feeling for the meaning of each. If you choose to, memorize the words as explained in "Mesmerizing Memorization Method".

Eccentric

(adj.) Not at or in the center; away from the center.
(adj.) Not perfectly circular; elliptical.
(adj.) Deviating from the norm; behaving unexpectedly or differently.

Interpret

(v.) To explain or tell the meaning of.
(v.) To translate orally into another language or terms.
(v.) To apprehend and represent by means of art.
(v.) To act as an interpreter.

Doctrine

(n.) A belief or tenet, especially about philosophical or theological (religious) matters.
(n.) A statement or belief of fundamental government policy.

Circumstance

(n.) Some thing or some abstract idea which attends, or relates to, or in some way affects, a fact or event.
(n.) An event; a fact; a particular incident.
(n.) Condition in regard to worldly estate; state of property; situation; surroundings.

Framework

(n.) A support structure comprising joined parts.
(adj.) The arrangement of support beams that represent a building's general shape and size.
(n.) A basic conceptual structure, as in government, computing, organizing.

Focus On: Vocabulary

B) Fill in the blanks with the correct word from this unit's words, make necessary structural changes to the word, then write the correct definition of the word being used on the line below the sentence.

1) He _____ at the meeting between the Chinese and French associates.
_____

2) The two boys found themselves in an unusual _____ when clowns surrounded them.
_____

3) The report provides a(n) _____ for further research.
_____

4) Open government is the governing _____ that government should be 100% transparent.
_____

5) Mars, Venus and the other planets move in _____ orbits.
_____

6) And Pharaoh told his dreams; but there was none that could _____ them unto Pharaoh.
_____

7) The four noble truths summarize the main _____ of Buddhism.
_____

9) The newly elected iconoclast chose _____, not centrist positions.
_____

10) The _____ are well known in the country where they happened.
_____

11) We just need a tent supported on a rigid _____.
_____

12) His _____ behavior lost him his job.
_____

13) An artist _____ a landscape.
_____

14) When men are easy in their _____, they are naturally enemies to innovations.
_____

15) This bridge over the river has a steel _____.
_____

16) I will attempt to _____ an Indian speech.
_____

C) Choose the correct definition from the word list page, then write it under the given paragraphs.

1) Everything about Cousin Mary's home was on a small scale. She herself was a very small and slight old lady, but she had inherited from the hardy New England race from which she sprang a certain tradition of vitality and longevity which she lived long enough to exemplify in her own person. Other family legends of **eccentric** ways and general worrisomeness she utterly disproved, for never was there a kindlier or more placid soul than she.

_____

_____

_____

2) I begged of them first to give me something to eat, and then I would satisfy their curiosity. They gave me several sorts of food, and when I had satisfied my hunger, I related all that had befallen me, which they listened to with attentive surprise. As soon as I had finished they told me, by the person who spoke Arabic and **interpreted** to them what I said, that I must go along with them, and tell my story to their king myself; it being too extraordinary to be related by any other than the person to whom the events had happened.

_____

_____

_____

3) So much for the spirit in which we should approach the problem, and I pass to the consideration of the problem itself. What is to be the **framework** of Home Rule? I take it for granted that there must, in the broad sense, be responsible government, that is to say, an Irish Legislature, with an Irish Cabinet responsible to that Legislature, and, through the Lord-Lieutenant, to the Crown.

(*Home Rule-The rule or government of a dependent country by the people within the country itself.)

_____

_____

_____

_____

4) It is not easy for anyone who has not been in the like condition to describe or conceive the consternation of men in such **circumstances**. We knew nothing of where we were, or upon what land it was we landed upon; whether an island or the main, whether inhabited or not inhabited. As the rage of the wind was still great, though rather less than at first, we could not so much as hope to have the ship hold many minutes without breaking in pieces, unless the winds, by a kind of miracle, should turn immediately about.

_____

_____

_____

5) That labor time is really the foundation of the exchangeable value of all things, excepting those which cannot be increased by human industry, is a **doctrine** of the utmost importance in politics; for from no source do so many errors, and so much difference of opinion in that science proceed, as from the vague ideas, which are attached to the word value.

_____

_____

_____

Unit 8:
Illustrate - Select - Suffrage - Focus - Response

A) Know the definitions - Read through each definition and get a feeling for the meaning of each. If you choose to, memorize the words as explained in "Mesmerizing Memorization Method".

Illustrate

(v.) To clarify something by giving, or serving as, an example or a comparison.
(v.) To draw; to provide a book or other publication with pictures, diagrams or other or decorative features.

Select

(adj.) Privileged, specially selected.
(adj.) Of high quality.
(v.) To choose one or more elements of a set, especially a set of options.

Suffrage

(n.) The right of women to vote.

Focus

(n.) A point at which reflected or refracted rays of light converge.
(n.) The most important part of something written or spoken, or the one that imparts information.
(n.) The exact point of where an earthquake occurs, in three dimensions.
(v.) To adjust (a lens, an optical instrument) in order to have an image proper, thin, clearly visible.
(v.) To concentrate one's attention.

Response

(n.) An answer or reply
(n.) The act of responding or replying; reply: as, to speak in response to a question.
(n.) A reply to an objection in a formal dispute.
(n.) A reaction to a stimulus or provocation.

Focus On: Vocabulary

B) Fill in the blanks with the correct word from this unit's words, make necessary structural changes to the word, then write the correct definition of the word being used on the line below the sentence.

1) This is a(n) _____ cut of beef that only our premier patrons receive.
_____

2) You need to _____ on passing the tests to maintain a 4.0 in this class.
_____

3) She used charts and diagrams to _____ the main points of her book's findings..
_____

4) He looked over the menu, and _____ the vegetarian platter.
_____

5) After taking the drug, his mind shut down and he gives no _____ to any stimuli.
_____

6) The professor's _____ in class to the question was very thought provoking.
_____

7) The _____ of the CEO's talk conveyed his enthusiasm for creating the best products.
_____

8) The U.S. passed legislation women's_____ in 1920.
_____

9) The company's bank statements _____ its continuous earnings.
_____

10) You'll need to _____ the microscope in order to capture the full detail of this surface.
_____

11) I've had no _____ to my email in weeks.
_____

12) The heat of sunlight at the _____ of a magnifying glass can set things on fire.
_____

13) The government has been cautious in its _____ to the negative report.
_____

14) Only a(n) _____ few received invitations to the ball.
_____

15) The earthquake's _____ was at exactly 37 ° north, 18 ° south.
_____

C) Choose the correct definition from the word list page, then write it under the given paragraphs.

1) Now I do not propose to dwell on the Renaissance and how Greek came in: for a number of writers in our time have been busy with the Renaissance, and have—I was going to say 'over-written the subject,' but no—it is better to say that they have **focused** the period so as to distort the general perspective at the cost of other periods which have earned less attention; e.g. the twelfth century. At any rate their efforts, with the amount they claim of your reading, absolve me from doing more than remind you that the Renaissance brought in the study of Greek, and Greek brought in the study of literature.

_____
_____
_____
_____

2) Aside from the higher motive of justice, we suggest your adoption of this principle of equal rights to women, as a means of securing your own future existence. The party of reform in this country is the party that lives. The party that ceases to represent the vital principles of truth and justice dies. If you would save the life of the Republican party, you should now take broad national ground on this question of **suffrage**.

_____
_____
_____

3) In the Australian Federal Parliament, the question was brought to an issue two or three years ago. Petitions bearing 200,000 signatures were presented to the parliament, and in **response,** a law was enacted absolutely prohibiting the importation of opium, except for medicinal uses. All the state governments of Australia lose revenue by this prohibition.

_____
_____
_____
_____

4) When instructing on a trees function to take in carbon dioxide and produce oxygen, it is important to point out the lenticels on the bark of birch and sweet cherry trees and explain how trees breathe. Compare this process with that of the human body. You may now come across an old stump, and here you can point out the structure of the wood—the sapwood, cambium, and bark. You can **illustrate** the annual rings and count the age of the tree. At another point, you may find a tree with a wound or bruised bark, and here you can readily make a closer study of the cambium layer and its manner of growth.

_____
_____
_____

5) But, independently of these or any other artificial monopolies, there is a natural monopoly in favor of skilled laborers against the unskilled, which makes the difference of reward exceed, sometimes in a manifold proportion, what is sufficient merely to equalize their advantages. But the fact that a course of instruction is required, or even a low degree of costliness, or that the laborer must be maintained for a considerable time from other sources, suffices everywhere to exclude the great body of the laboring people from the possibility of any such competition. Until lately, all employments which required even the humble education of reading and writing could be recruited only from a **select** class, the majority having had no opportunity of acquiring those attainments.

_____
_____
_____

Focus On: Vocabulary

Unit 9:
Convert - Compute - Substantiate - Project - Immigrate

A) Know the definitions - Read through each definition and get a feeling for the meaning of each. If you choose to, memorize the words as explained in "Mesmerizing Memorization Method".

Convert

(n.) A person who is now in favor of something that he or she previously opposed or disliked.
(v.) To transform or change (something) into another form, substance, state, or product.
(v.) To change (something) from one use, function, or purpose to another.
(v.) To induce (someone) to adopt a particular religion, faith, ideology or belief.
(v.) To exchange for something of equal value, as in units of measurement or money.

Compute

(v.) To calculate.
(v.) To make sense.

Substantiate

(v.) To verify something by supplying evidence; to authenticate or corroborate.
(v.) To give material form or substance to something; to embody; to record in documents.

Project

(n.) A planned endeavor, usually with a specific goal and accomplished in several steps or stages.
(n.) An urban low-income housing building.
(v.) To extend beyond a surface.
(v.) To cast (an image or shadow) upon a surface; to throw or cast forward; to shoot forth.
(v.) To make plans for; to forecast.
(v.) To send out feelings to keep people out.

Immigrate

(v.) To move into a country from another one to stay permanently.

Focus On: Vocabulary

B) Fill in the blanks with the correct word from this unit's words, make necessary structural changes to the word, then write the correct definition of the word being used on the line below the sentence.

1) The manager entered into the _____ with unusual zeal.
_____

2) The CEO is _____ the completion of the new power plant by next spring.
_____

3) I never really liked broccoli before, but now that I've tasted it with cheese, I'm a(n) _____!
_____

4) The records of the court _____ the fact that the property originally belonged to his family.
_____

5) Water _____ into steam.
_____

6) Housing _____ are found in metropolitan areas.
_____

7) That doesn't _____, can you explain further?
_____

8) Our ancestors _____ here almost three hundred years ago.
_____

9) He _____ his sunroom into a library.
_____

10) The new solar shingles do not _____ beyond the houses' outer walls like the old ones did.
_____

11) The lawyers have evidence to _____ the allegations against him.
_____

12) _____ emotions onto others is something we all do to some degree.
_____

13) They _____ her to Christianity before she died.
_____

14) I can _____ the square root of 1,000,000, it's 1000.
_____

15) The sun _____ long shadows at this time of day.
_____

16) We _____ our US dollars into Bitcoins.
_____

C) Choose the correct definition from the word list page, then write it under the given paragraphs.

1) Hoosac Mountain was the chief obstacle in the path of a railroad **projected** between Greenfield, Massachusetts, and Troy, New York. The line was launched by a group of Boston merchants to provide a direct route to the rapidly developing West, in competition with the coastal routes via New York. The only route economically reasonable included a tunnel of nearly five miles through the mountain—a length absolutely without precedent, and an immense undertaking in view of the relatively primitive rock-working methods then available.

_____

_____

_____

2) This entry gives the gross domestic product (GDP) or value of all final goods and services produced within a nation in a given year. A nation's GDP at official exchange rates (OER) is the home-currency-denominated annual GDP figure divided by the bilateral average US exchange rate with that country in that year. The measure is simple to **compute** and gives a precise measure of the value of output. Many economists prefer this measure when gauging the economic power an economy maintains.

_____

_____

_____

3) When it was first reported that Steve Holcombe, one of the most successful, daring and famous gamblers in the South, had been **converted** and had joined the church, the usual predictions were made that in less than three months, etc., he would see his mistake or yield to discouragements and return to his old life of self-indulgence and ease. But when men passed and repassed the corner where this man had a little fruit store and was trying to make an honest living for his family, their thoughts became more serious and their questions deepen Steve had got something or something had got him.

_____

_____

_____

4) Although the majority of pig sellers may claim to be, and may be able to **substantiate** the claim to be, equally as honest as the majority of others in trade, yet there may be a small minority who are apt to attempt to palm off pigs as being older than they really are. It is most annoying when you are anxious to purchase pigs of say six or seven months old which are quite ready to be quickly fattened, to have pigs of four or five months old which continue to make growth instead of flesh, so that they are not ready for killing until two or three months after they are required for conversion into bacon.

_____

_____

_____

5) When possible, it is ideal for people who are in a tough state of life in their native lands to **immigrate** to a nation that will allow more opportunities for them and their families. These opportunities include better work, higher education standards, and a more convenient lifestyle. By making the "big move", those brave individuals secure a better life for themselves as well as for their subsequent generations. This has been a normal process for people since perhaps the dawn of man.

_____

_____

_____

Unit 10:
Constant - Label - Participate - Dominion - Initial

A) Know the definitions - Read through each definition and get a feeling for the meaning of each. If you choose to, memorize the words as explained in "Mesmerizing Memorization Method".

Constant

(adj.) Unchanged through time or space; permanent.
(adj.) Consistently recurring over time; persistent.
(adj.) Steady in purpose, action, feeling, etc.
(adj.) Firm; solid; not fluid.
(n.) Any property of an experiment, determined numerically, that does not change under circumstances.

Label

(n.) A small ticket or sign giving information about something which is attached.
(n.) A name given to something or someone to categorize them as part of a particular social group.
(n.) A company that sells records.
(v.) To put a label (a ticket or sign) on (something).
(v.) To give a label to (someone or something) in order to categorize that person or thing.

Participate

(v.) To join in; to take part.

Dominion

(n.) Power or the use of power; ultimate authority.
(n.) A kingdom, nation, or governed territory.
(n.) Common or widespread; significant or important; dominant.

Initial

(adj.) Chronologically first, early; of or pertaining to the beginning.
(adj.) Spatially first; placed at the beginning; in the first position.

Focus On: Vocabulary

B) Fill in the blanks with the correct word from this unit's words, make necessary structural changes to the word, then write the correct definition of the word being used on the line below the sentence.

1) I am _____ to my current goals in life.
_____

2) The manager _____ all the products in the store.
_____

3) Dictators had complete _____ over all of their subjects until most were overthrown.
_____

4) The _____ given to everyone in the computer room during lunch is "nerd".
_____

5) King Arthur's _____ was over Camelot.
_____

6) When she turned, we laughed at her because the _____ was still on her new sweater.
_____

7) In the experiment, the _____ was the water and the variables were the solutes.
_____

8) The teachers _____ in the school parade with the students.
_____

9) The _____ version of the program had some bugs that had to be debugged.
_____

10) The _____ signed the band after hearing a demo tape.
_____

11) Oceanic climates have frequent cloudy conditions due to the near _____ storms.
_____

12) Objects placed foremost usually have _____ over things behind them.
_____

13) The _____ distractions of electronic devices are causing people subliminal stress.
_____

14) On the _____ test, I scored poorly, but I'll do better on the second one.
_____

15) Nill has been _____ as a bum, ever since he asked his friends for money.
_____

16) If you mix these two fluid liquids, you may turn them into a(n) _____ body.
_____

C) Choose the correct definition from the word list page, then write it under the given paragraphs.

1) The sequence of day and night is a phenomenon belonging, properly speaking, to the Earth, in which the rest of the Universe does not **participate**. The same occurs for every world that is illuminated by a sun, and endowed with a rotary movement. In absolute space, there is no succession of nights and days.

_____

_____

_____

_____

2) The kind of society which encourages creative self-expression, independent judgment and a living expanding fellowship must necessarily be conceived and created in freedom. For to these essential human impulses, freedom is the very breath of life. The **initial** problem of sociology is, therefore, the achievement of freedom; upon that foundation, and that only, can it build for eternity.

_____

_____

_____

_____

3) The distance between two points is to be the length measured with a rigid scale. Let us mark the two points by particles of matter because we must somehow identify them by reference to material objects. For simplicity, we shall suppose that the two particles have no relative motion so that the distance—whatever it is—remains a **constant**. Now you will probably agree that there is no such thing as absolute motion; consequently, there is no standard condition of the scale which we can call "at rest."

_____

_____

_____

_____

4) I was curious to know how this prince, to whose lands there is no access from any other country, came to think of armies, or to teach his people the practice of military discipline. But I was soon informed, both by conversation and reading their histories. In the course of many ages, they have been troubled with the same disease to which the whole race of mankind is subject; the nobility often contending for power, the people for liberty, and the king for absolute **dominion**.

_____

_____

_____

_____

5) Civilization is the progressive mastery of its varied energies. When this interdependence of the study of history, representing the human emphasis, with the study of geography, representing the natural, is ignored, history sinks to a listing of dates with an appended inventory of events, **labeled** "important"; or else it becomes a literary phantasy—for in purely literary history the natural environment is but stage scenery.

_____

_____

_____

_____

Unit 6-10 Review

Match the correct definition with the correct word by writing the correct definition' letter in the blank next to the word that corresponds to that definition.

_____1. Taut   A. Of high quality

_____2. Eccentric   B. A name given to something or someone to categorize them as part of a particular social group.

_____3. Doctrine   C. Marked by diversity or difference.

_____4. Project   D. Steady in purpose, action, feeling, etc.

_____5. Constant   E. A point at which reflected or refracted rays of light converge.

_____6. Variable   F. A person who is now in favor of something that he or she previously opposed

_____7. Label   G. Behaving unexpectedly or differently

_____8. Select   H. To make plans for

_____9. Convert   I. Containing only relevant parts

_____10. Focus   J. a statement or belief of fundamental government

Fill in the blanks with the correct word from this unit's words:

The _____ for a good college course requires a well-structured and _____ curriculum that covers all relevant topics for the subject. From the professor's _____ meeting with the students, he or she must present an adequate syllabus and build rapport with the students, assuring them that he or she is organized and knowledgeable. It is important to _____ this type of first impression which will establish the professor's position and encourage class participation later on in the semester. Though the personalities of the students are a _____ out of the professor's control, the professor should do what he or she can to put his or her best foot forward and prepare the students for a great semester.

Unit 11:
Available - Commit - Perceive - Dimension - Minor

A) Know the definitions - Read through each definition and get a feeling for the meaning of each. If you choose to, memorize the words as explained in "Mesmerizing Memorization Method".

Available

(adj.) Capable of being used for a purpose.
(adj.) Readily obtainable.
(adj.) Not in a romantic relationship; single.

Commit

(v.) To give in trust; to put into charge or keeping; to entrust.
(v.) To put in charge of a jailer; to imprison; To incarcerate a person into a prison.
(v.) To have entered an establishment, such as a hospital or asylum, as a patient.
(v.) To do (something bad); to perpetrate, as a crime, sin.
(v.) To pledge or bind to some act.

Perceive

(v.) To become aware of, through the physical senses or by thinking; to see; to understand.

Dimension

(n.) A single aspect of a given thing.
(n.) A measure of spatial extent in a particular direction, such as height, width or breadth, or depth.
(n.) An alternative universe or plane of existence.

Minor

(adj.) Of little significance or importance.
(adj.) Of a scale which has lowered scale degrees three, six, and seven relative to major, but with the sixth and seventh not always lowered.
(n.) A person who is below the legal age of majority, consent, criminal responsibility.
(n.) A subject area of secondary concentration of a student at a college or university.
(v.) To choose or have an area of secondary concentration as a student in a college or university.

Focus On: Vocabulary

B) Fill in the blanks with the correct word from this unit's words, make necessary structural changes to the word, then write the correct definition of the word being used on the line below the sentence.

1. The detective solved the identity of the perpetrator before he could _____ another crime.
   _____

2. Voters _____ him as a charismatic and capable presidential candidate.
   _____

3. I asked her if she was _____ but she said she had a boyfriend.
   _____

4. I _____ in French, but majored in German.
   _____

5. These criminals were _____ to prison for "rehabilitation".
   _____

6. The list shows the _____ products in the store.
   _____

7. The physical appearance of a singer is a(n) _____ factor to music fans.
   _____

8. Kerry should be _____ to a nuthouse for the way she's been acting!
   _____

9. _____ under the age of eighteen cannot be drafted to war.
   _____

10. I will _____ myself to ending world hunger.
    _____

11. There is another _____ to this problem that needs to be solved.
    _____

12. Bid him farewell, _____ him to the grave.
    _____

13. We live our lives in three _____ .
    _____

14. The jazz _____ scale is a derivative of the melodic minor scale.
    _____

15. Our company has a(n) _____ delivery man to send to your office.
    _____

16. She became an English _____ .
    _____

17. Scientists are working on creating a device which will allow people to go to other _____ .
    _____

C) Choose the correct definition from the word list page, then write it under the given paragraphs.

1) 'Ah, you should have thought of that before. Otherwise, I have **committed** myself for nothing.

''Yes, I should have thought of it,' he answered gravely. 'But I did not. There lies my fault; I admit it freely. Ah, if you would only commit yourself a little more, I might at least get over that difficulty! But I won't ask you. You have no idea how much you are to me still; you could not argue so coolly if you had.'

_____

_____

_____

2) Wisely or foolishly, Mademoiselle V--- came to a resolution: that her only safety lay in flight. His contiguity influenced her too sensibly; she could not reason. So packing up her few possessions and placing on the table the small sum she owed, she went out privately, secured a last **available** seat in the London coach, and, almost before she had fully weighed her action, she was rolling out of the town in the dusk of the September evening.

_____

_____

_____

3) After the ribs are all in place and the framework completed, turn the canoe upside down upon the wooden horses—for a canoe as large as the one needed for 6, you will need three horses, one at each end and one in the middle. For a canoe of the **dimensions** with sixteen feet inside measurement, you would need about seven yards of ten-ounce cotton canvas, of sufficient width to reach up over the sides of your canoe. Take a tape-measure or a piece of ordinary tape or a long strip of manila paper and measure around the bottom of the boat at its widest part in the middle from one gunwale (top of side) to the other, and see that your cloth is fully as wide as your measurement.

_____

_____

_____

_____

4) Apart from **minor** grounds on which Kant's philosophy may be criticized, there is one main objection which seems fatal to any attempt to deal with the problem of a priori knowledge by his method. The thing to be accounted for is our certainty that the facts must always conform to logic and arithmetic. To say that logic and arithmetic are contributed by us does not account for this. Our nature is as much a fact of the existing world as anything, and there can be no certainty that it will remain constant.

_____

_____

_____

5) Realities mean either concrete facts, or abstract kinds of things and relations **perceived** intuitively between them. They furthermore and thirdly mean, as things that new ideas of ours must no less take account of, the whole body of other truths already in our possession. But what now does 'agreement' with such three-fold realities mean?—to use again the definition that is current.

_____

_____

_____

Unit 12:
Contrast - Resolution - Egregious - Phase - Dismay

A) Know the definitions - Read through each definition and get a feeling for the meaning of each. If you choose to, memorize the words as explained in "Mesmerizing Memorization Method".

Contrast

(n.) A difference in lightness, brightness and/or hue between two colors that makes them more or less distinguishable.
(n.) A difference between two objects, people or concepts.
(v.) To set in opposition in order to show the difference or differences between.

Resolution

(n.) A strong will; determination.
(n.) Firmness in intent.
(n.) A statement of intent; a vow.
(n.) The degree of fineness with which an image can be recorded or produced.
(n.) The act or process of solving in math; solution.
(n.) A formal statement adopted by an assembly, or during any other formal meeting.
(n.) The moment in which the conflict ends and the outcome of the action is clear.

Egregious

(adj.) Noticeable in a bad way.

Phase

(n.) A distinguishable part of a sequence or cycle occurring over time.
(n.) How something appears to the eye, especially with different and varying appearances of the same object.
(n.) A particular appearance or state in a regularly recurring cycle of changes in the moon's brightness or form.
(n.) Chemical composition and/or physical state (solid, liquid or gas) and/or crystal structure.

Dismay

(n.) A sudden or complete loss of courage and firmness in the face of trouble or danger.

Focus On: Vocabulary

B) Fill in the blanks with the correct word from this unit's words, make necessary structural changes to the word, then write the correct definition of the word being used on the line below the sentence.

1. The loss of his key supporter did not stagger his _____ to campaign for governor.
_____

2. The red and the orange don't have much _____ between them.
_____

3. The injury to their quarterback caused the team's _____.
_____

4. The novel is about how the writer _____ good with evil.
_____

5. My New Year's _____ is to exercise at least once a month this year.
_____

6. The nervous student made _____ errors on every single test he took.
_____

7. The three most common states or, _____, of matter are: solid, liquid, and gas.
_____

8. The photo's _____ is too blurry, so printing it a this size won't look good.
_____

9. There are eight _____ of the moon.
_____

10. The student received enough help from his teacher to get the _____ for the equation.
_____

11. Without the lawyer's advice, a(n) _____ for the contract could not have been made.
_____

12. The first _____ of project is projected to be finished by December.
_____

13. The traveler's reentry _____ varied in levels of clarity during the teleportation test.
_____

14. The United States of America is a country of many _____.
_____

15. A majority vote enabled the passage of the _____.
_____

C) Choose the correct definition from the word list page, then write it under the given paragraphs.

1) The objects best delineated on these photographic papers, are lace, feathers, dried plants, particularly the ferns, sea-weeds and the light grasses, impressions of copper plate and wood engravings, particularly if they have considerable **contrast** of light and shade. These should be placed with the face downwards, having been previously prepared as directed.

_____

_____

_____

2) I felt faint and cold when I faced the empty space among the black tangle of bushes. I ran around it furiously, as if the thing might be hidden in a corner, and then stopped abruptly, with my hands clutching my hair. Above me towered the sphinx, upon the bronze pedestal, white, shining, leprous, in the light of the rising moon. It seemed to smile in mockery of my **dismay**.

_____

_____

_____

3) The last child, Tom, was considerably younger than his brothers, so had belonged rather to the company of his sisters. He was his mother's favorite. She roused herself to determination and sent him forcibly away to a grammar-school in Derby when he was twelve years old. He did not want to go, and his father would have given way, but Mrs. Brangwen had set her heart on it. Her slender, pretty, tightly-covered body, with full skirts, was now the center of **resolution** in the house, and when she had once set upon anything, which was not often, the family failed before her.

_____

_____

_____

4) The capacity of New York City to undertake the work had been much discussed in the courts, and the Supreme Court of the State had disposed of the debt allowance discussion **phase** of the situation by suggesting that it did not make much difference to the municipality whether or not the debt limit permitted a contract for the work, because if the limit should be exceeded, "no liability could possibly be imposed upon the city," a view which might comfort the timid taxpayers but could hardly be expected to give confidence to the capitalists who might undertake the execution of the contract.

_____

_____

_____

5) Fortunately, the cooking of spinach is the simplest of culinary devices. While the fresh green leaves were sinking to a pulp in the earthen pipkin, I had the privilege of watching the señora make one of her excellent omelets—an invaluable lesson. Though I gave it a try, this attempt will render impossible my again making such an **egregious** failure as I did when attempting to cook an omelet in the same fashion.

_____

_____

_____

Unit 13:
Research - Stress - Predict - Coordinate - Negate

A) Know the definitions - Read through each definition and get a feeling for the meaning of each. If you choose to, memorize the words as explained in "Mesmerizing Memorization Method".

Research

(n.) In-depth inquiry or examination to seek or revise facts, principles, theories, applications.
(n.) A particular instance or piece of research.
(v.) To search or examine with continued care; to seek diligently.
(v.) To make an extensive investigation into.

Stress

(n.) Force externally applied to a body or structure which causes internal stress within the body.
(n.) Emotional pressure suffered by a human being or other animal.
(n.) The emphasis placed on a syllable of a word.
(v.) To emphasize (a point) in an argument or discussion.

Predict

(v.) To forecast; foretell; tell the future.

Coordinate

(n.) A number representing the position of a point along a line, arc, or similar one-dimensional figure.
(v.) To cause two or more events to happen at exactly the same time.

Negate

(v.) To deny the existence, evidence, or truth of.
(v.) To make have no value or cause to be ineffective.
(v.) To be negative; bring or cause negative results.

Focus On: Vocabulary

B) Fill in the blanks with the correct word from this unit's words, make necessary structural changes to the word, then write the correct definition of the word being used on the line below the sentence.

1) Scientific _____ is necessary to make new innovations.
_____

2) Progress on the project has been _____ by the lack of interest by the participants.
_____

3) People put the _____ on the first syllables of words to make a point when speaking.
_____

4) Our teachers _____ activities with those of other schools.
_____

5) Prof. Xi is _____ into the reading problems of pupils.
_____

6) Earthquakes happen when _____ in rock are suddenly released.
_____

7) The _____ X and Y need to be written on the graph.
_____

8) He's been under a lot of _____ these days.
_____

9) Years of extensive work went into _____ his book of wonders.
_____

10) Atheists _____ the existence of God.
_____

11) Numerous _____ have been made on the differentiation of poison dart frogs.
_____

12) I must _____ that this mission is top secret and cannot be discussed with anyone.
_____

13) Timmy has an attitude that always_____ the bad vibes of his classmates.
_____

14) No one can _____ what will happen next.
_____

C) Choose the correct definition from the word list page, then write it under the given paragraphs.

1) An instant the brown-flecked eyes appeared to be searching for some human contact which she seemed vaguely to have lost. And then she began at the beginning—with her daughter's engagement to young Andrew McCrae, her happiness, her security—and quietly, with only now and then a slight tension of her body and her voice, she told it all to them, exactly as it happened, without plea or embellishment. She had only one **stress**, and that she tried to make understandable to them—her child's security.

_____

_____

_____

2) Modern dairying is attempting to build its more accurate knowledge upon a broader and surer foundation, and in doing this is seeking to ascertain the cause of well-established processes. In this, bacteriology is playing an important role. It may be safely predicted that future progress in dairying will greatly depend upon bacteriological **research**. As Fleischmann, the eminent German dairy scientist says: "The gradual abolition of uncertainty surrounding dairy manufacture is the present important duty which lies before us, and its solution can only be affected by bacteriology."

_____

_____

_____

3) John Dalton's apparatus consisted of rude home-made rain-gauges, thermometers, and barometers. His interest in the heat, moisture, and constituents of the atmosphere continued throughout life, and Dalton made in all some 200,000 meteorological observations. We gain a clue to his motive in these studies from a letter written when he was twenty-two years old, in which he speaks of the advantages that might benefit the farmer, the mariner, and to mankind in general if we were able to **predict** the state of the weather with tolerable precision.

_____

_____

_____

4) Within the past year, many of our industrialists have come to the conclusion that since the great decline of our export trade, the chief hope of industrial rehabilitation lies in a workable and important method of dealing with farm surpluses. Support for the trial of some plan to put the tariff into effect seems to be found everywhere now. It will be my purpose to compose the conflicting elements of these various plans, to gather the benefit of the long study and consideration of them, to **coordinate** efforts to the end that agreement may be reached upon the details of a distinct policy to restore agriculture to economic equality with other industry.

_____

_____

_____

5) The farm woman's most demanding task probably centered around the preparation and preservation of food, a vitally important function, because to waste or misuse food was to **negate** the hard labor of a year. In the current era of convenience foods, the time-consuming nature of cooking is easily forgotten. Just operating a microwave oven, a simple entering in of four numbers, can cook foods which can be done within seconds after the task is set to.

_____

_____

_____

Unit 14:
Ignorance - Ponder - Set - Enable - Pragmatic

A) Know the definitions - Read through each definition and get a feeling for the meaning of each. If you choose to, memorize the words as explained in "Mesmerizing Memorization Method".

Ignorance

(n.) The condition of being uninformed or uneducated.

Ponder

(v.) To wonder; to think of deeply.
(v.) To consider (something) carefully and thoroughly.

Set

(v.) To put (something) down.
(v.) To focus attention on something.
(v.) To determine or settle.
(v.) To arrange with dishes and cutlery; to set the table.
(v.) To introduce or describe.
(v.) To devise and assign (work) to.
(v.) To solidify; to become solid.
(v.) To place plants or shoots in the ground; to plant.

Enable

(v.) To give strength or ability to; to make firm and strong.
(v.) To make something possible.
(v.) To allow a way out or excuse for an action.

Pragmatic

(adj.) Practical, useful in practice, not just theory.

Focus On: Vocabulary

B) Fill in the blanks with the correct word from this unit's words, make necessary structural changes to the word, then write the correct definition of the word being used on the line below the sentence.

1) Marie, please _____ the table for eight dinner guests.
   _____

2) The money will _____ us to restore the windows of the library.
   _____

3) I will take some time and _____ the questions before answering them on today's test.
   _____

4) I'll _____ the vase beside the window.
   _____

5) The data will _____ us to construct a profile of the firm's customers.
   _____

6) I am _____ on participating in the school play.
   _____

7) My parents are _____ about how they spend their money.
   _____

8) The owners of the apartment complex _____ the rent at affordable prices.
   _____

9) Knowledge makes humble; _____ makes proud.
   _____

10) The author _____ the characters in a chaotic situation for conflict resolution.
    _____

11) I have spent days _____ the meaning of life.
    _____

12) The mixture _____ on the model's face and neck to create a perfect bust.
    _____

13) His parents _____ him to continue gambling by giving him access to their bank account.
    _____

14) The teacher _____ the students to the task of writing an original play.
    _____

15) Our neighbor always _____ his tomato plants as soon as the last frost is gone.
    _____

C) Choose the correct definition from the word list page, then write it under the given paragraphs.

1) Our health so far had remained excellent—lime juice well offsetting the steady diet of tinned and salted food, and temperatures generally above zero **enabling** us to do without our thickest furs. It was now midsummer, and with haste and care, we might be able to conclude work by March and avoid a tedious wintering through the long Antarctic night. Several savage windstorms had burst upon us from the west, but we had escaped damage through the skill of Atwood in devising rudimentary shelters and windbreaks of heavy snow blocks and reinforcing the principal camp buildings with snow.

_____

_____

_____

2) The influence on history of the invention of the science of astronomy has been so great that we cannot estimate its greatness. On it the whole science of navigation rests. Without it, the science and the art of navigation could not exist, no ships could cross the ocean from one port to another, except by accident, and the lands that are separated by the ocean would still rest in complete **ignorance** of each other. This world would not be a world, but only a widely separated number of barbarian countries; most of them as ignorant of even the existence of the others as in the days before Columbus.

_____

_____

_____

3) "That's what she has," said Andrew firmly. "That's what she has, and Ms. Dobson has **set** her mind on it—and I never refuse her nothin'. I don't want nothin' to reproach myself for. You went off and left that girl—the finest girl in town—and near about broke her heart. You ought to be ashamed now."

_____

_____

_____

4) Possibly **pragmatic** writers are to blame for the tendency of their critics to assume that the practice they have in mind is utilitarian in some narrow sense, referring to some preconceived and inferior use. But what the pragmatic theory has in mind is precisely the fact that all the affairs of life which need regulation—all values of all types—depend upon utilizations of meanings. Action is not to be limited to anything less than the carrying out of ideas, than the execution, whether strenuous or easeful, of meanings.

_____

_____

_____

5) As I sat there in the National Museum of Space, I **pondered** the millions, perhaps billions of people who stared up at the sky and thought whether there was something besides ourselves out there. Not that I myself wondered if there was extraterrestrial life off of Mother Earth, I just mulled the idea of all the people before me thinking about it. Why had it taken until now for man to achieve off-world capabilities? If so many before me thought of space, then somebody should have come up with a way to achieve it, but no, it took until now.

_____

_____

_____

Unit 15:
Specify - Grant - Prior - Symbol - Transit

A) Know the definitions - Read through each definition and get a feeling for the meaning of each. If you choose to, memorize the words as explained in "Mesmerizing Memorization Method".

Specify

(v.) To state explicitly, or in detail.

Grant

(v.) To give (permission or wish).
(v.) To admit as true what is not yet satisfactorily proved.
(v.) To assent; to consent; to agree to.
(n.) Money, property or some thing granted; a gift; a boon.
(n.) A transfer of property by deed or writing.
(n.) The deed or writing by which such a transfer (of land or money) is made.

Prior

(n.) A high-ranking member of a monastery (building for housing monks).
(n.) A previous arrest or criminal conviction on someone's record.
(adj.) Previous; coming before.
(Adv) Previously.

Symbol

(n.) A character or glyph representing an idea, concept or object.
(n.) Any object, typically material, which is meant to represent another.
(n.) An authoritative summary of religion, faith or doctrine.

Transit

(v.) To pass over, across or through something.
(n.) The moving of people or goods, especially on a public transportation system.

Focus On: Vocabulary

B) Fill in the blanks with the correct word from this unit's words, make necessary structural changes to the word, then write the correct definition of the word being used on the line below the sentence.

1) The police got the report on his prints, and he already had a(n) _____ for attempted robbery.
_____

2) The _____ # is commonly known as the hash tag or the number sign.
_____

3) I _____, for the sake of argument, that science may have more answers than religion has.
_____

4) The dollar _____ has no relationship to the concept of currency or any related idea.
_____

5) Our group was given a(n) _____ of land for experimental agriculture purposes.
_____

6) The boss didn't _____ what time the meeting would be held.
_____

7) Students must satisfy certain criteria to qualify for a(n) _____.
_____

8) The _____ gave service daily to the monks in the monastery's chapel.
_____

9) Trucks are the primary form of _____ of goods through a country.
_____

10) Test takers should not rely on _____ knowledge when taking certain standardized exams.
_____

11) Only a handful of countries would _____ him political asylum.
_____

12) The CEO had known two months _____ that major layoffs were coming.
_____

13) The Bible is one of the _____ of Christianity.
_____

14) He was _____ permission to attend the meeting.
_____

15) The train crossed numerous bridges to _____ the continent.
_____

16) We submitted the _____ to the government six months ago.
_____

C) Choose the correct definition from the word list page, then write it under the given paragraphs.

1) Under the bill, as amended by my friend from Minnesota, nine-tenths of the land is open to actual settlers at $250.00 per acre; the remaining one-tenth is pine-timbered land, that is not fit for settlement, and never will be settled upon; but the timber will be cut off. I admit that it is the most valuable portion of the **grant**. It is quite valueless; and if you put in this amendment of the gentleman from Indiana, you may as well just kill the bill, because no man and no company will build the road in the wilderness due to the terribly hard work needed in doing so.

_____

_____

_____

2) Having once recognized that the **symbols** stood for letters, and having applied the rules which guide us in all forms of secret writings, the solution was easy enough. The first message submitted to me was so short that it was impossible for me to do more than to say, with some confidence, that the symbol ZZZ stood for E. As most are aware, E is the most common letter in the English alphabet, and it predominates to so marked an extent that even in a short sentence one would expect to find it most often.

_____

_____

_____

3) As we loaded the trucks, the foreman stopped and thought about something for what seemed a long time. Who knows what he really thought about but he told us that all **prior** shipments were checked individually by the delivery people and that we just had to unload them onto the docks. I thought I could almost hear a sigh of relief from every one of my coworkers after her said that.

_____

_____

_____

_____

4) The completion of the rapid **transit** railroad in the boroughs of Manhattan and The Bronx, which is popularly known as the "Subway," has demonstrated that underground railroads can be built beneath the congested streets of the city. This accomplishment has made possible in the near future a comprehensive system of subsurface transportation extending throughout the wide territory of Greater New York.

_____

_____

_____

_____

5) I've dealt with this company several times before and each time has been a headache. None of the representatives there seem able to give a helpful suggestion on what we really need as a company based on industry standards. The thing that really gets me is when I don't even know what I want and they ask me to **specify** on what we want to order. How can I do that when I don't even know what we need?!

_____

_____

_____

_____

Unit 11-15 Review

Match the correct definition with the correct word by writing the correct definition' letter in the blank next to the word that corresponds to that definition.

_____ 1. Resolution   A. A subject area of secondary concentration of a student at a college or university

_____ 2. Commit   B. To think of deeply

_____ 3. Grant   C. To apply force to (a body or structure) causing strain.

_____ 4. Coordinate   D. To become solid

_____ 5. Prior   E. The deed or writing by which such a transfer (of land or money) is made.

_____ 6. Stress   F. A vow

_____ 7. Phase   G. Coming before

_____ 8. Minor   H. To give in trust

_____ 9. Ponder   I. To cause two or more events to happen at exactly the same time.

_____ 10. Set   J. How something appears to the eye, especially with different and varying appearances of the same object.

Fill in the blanks with the correct word from this unit's words:

To his _____, James _____ that Mrs. Angelo was not fond of him for some reason. He could tell this from the harsh tone of her voice towards him, the glares she shot at him in class, and how she _____ everything he said, even if it was a fact. She made her disdain for him quite obvious to the entire class as well. He _____ different ways he could try to win her favor before the school year ended, and wondered if perhaps he could write her a thank you card and gift her some chocolates as _____ of his appreciation to her for being his teacher. For now, all he could do was be on his best behavior and stay out of trouble.

Unit 16:
Environment - Dominate - Undermine - Objective - Subjective

A) Know the definitions - Read through each definition and get a feeling for the meaning of each. If you choose to, memorize the words as explained in "Mesmerizing Memorization Method".

Environment

(n.) The surroundings of, and influences on someone or something.
(n.) The natural world or ecosystem.
(n.) A particular political or social setting, arena or condition.
(n.) The software and/or hardware existing on any particular computer system.

Dominate

(v.) To govern, rule or control by superior authority or power.
(v.) To exert an overwhelming guiding influence over something or someone.
(v.) To enjoy a commanding position in some field.
(v.) To overlook from a height.
(v.) To be the most frequent or common.

Undermine

(n.) To weaken or work against; to hinder; sabotage.

Objective

(adj.) Not influenced by personal feelings or opinions in considering and representing facts.
(adj.) Not necessary based on the mind or thought for existence; actual.
(n.) A goal that effort is required.
(n.) The goal of a military operation.

Subjective

(adj.) Formed, as in opinions, based on a person's feelings or intuition, not on observation or reasoning.

Focus On: Vocabulary

B) Fill in the blanks with the correct word from this unit's words, make necessary structural changes to the word, then write the correct definition of the word being used on the line below the sentence.

1) Technological professions _____ most fields in modern nations.
_____

2) Our current _____ is to take and hold that hill from the enemy.
_____

3) The religious _____ of pre-Renaissance Europe dominated most aspects of people's lives.
_____

4) The rebels now _____ the country after winning most of the battles in their civil war.
_____

5) The Microsoft Windows _____ is on most personal computers.
_____

6) His wife _____ his authority by disagreeing with his methods of disciplining the children.
_____

7) Pine trees _____ the forest near my house upstate.
_____

8) Judges try to be _____ and impartial when judging cases in a court of law.
_____

9) His overbearing will was such that he _____ the other advisors in the President's cabinet.
_____

10) Everyone's opinion is _____ because of their own ideas and biases which are different.
_____

11) _____ laws take biased thought out of criminal cases, so the punishment fits the crime.
_____

12) James requires a silent and serene _____ to write his novels.
_____

13) The Sahara Desert is a hostile _____ for anyone so unfortunate to be left to its mercy.
_____

14) The Eiffel Tower _____ the skyline of Paris.
_____

15) We will use every possible means to achieve our _____.
_____

C) Choose the correct definition from the word list page, then write it under the given paragraphs.

1) Writing is a process where a student learns to write mainly by reading texts in the formative years of elementary school, then puts it to use in middle school, and much more in high school. Teachers demonstrate that **subjective** creativity in student's writing can be influenced by what interests the student. The more that a student reads of a certain genre, the more that student will emulate it. Therefore, it is essential for students to read a variety of texts to get a well-rounded sense of literacy.

_____

_____

_____

2) They must not give up what was right for a little money—if they did, the money would never do them any good, they could depend upon that. And Elzbieta would call upon Dede Antanas to support her; there was a fear in the souls of these two, unless this journey to a new country might somehow **undermine** the old home virtues of their children.

_____

_____

_____

3) For that moment I touched an emotion beyond the common range of men, yet one that the poor brutes we **dominate** know only too well. I felt as a rabbit might feel returning to his burrow and suddenly confronted by the work of a dozen busy navvies digging the foundations of a house. I felt the first inkling of a thing that grew clear in my mind, that oppressed me for many days, a sense of dethronement, a persuasion that I was no longer a master, but an animal among the animals, under the Martian heel. With us it would be as with them, to lurk and watch, to run and hide.

_____

_____

_____

4) The Harmonist of the Renaissance is Raphael Sanzio's title. And this harmony extended to a blending of thought, form, and expression, heightening or modifying every element until they ran together with such rhythm that it could not be seen where one left off and another began. He was the very opposite of Michael Angelo. The art of the latter was an expression of individual power and was purely subjective. Raphael's art was largely a unity of **objective** beauties, with the personal element as much in abeyance as was possible for his time.

_____

_____

_____

5) The nineteenth century saw the initiation of great changes in the economic **environment** due to the rapid invention of machinery. This, with the equally rapid application of steam power, led to an increase of wealth production never before known on the earth. During the same period, new modes of transport were brought into daily use, the facilities for inter-communication were increased a hundred-fold, scientific discoveries opened up to us new and unthought-of mysteries of the universe, and the whole earth was ransacked for its treasures.

_____

_____

_____

Unit 17:
Migrate - Integrate - Series - Draft - Contend

A) **Know the definitions** - Read through each definition and get a feeling for the meaning of each. If you choose to, memorize the words as explained in "Mesmerizing Memorization Method".

Migrate

(v.) To relocate periodically from one region to another.
(v.) To change one's geographic pattern of habitation.
(v.) To move slowly towards, usually in groups.
(v.) To move computer code or files from one computer or network to another.

Integrate

(v.) To form into one whole; to make entire; to complete.
(v.) To include as a constituent part or functionality.
(v.) To desegregate, as a school or neighborhood.

Series

(n.) A number of things that follow on one after the other or are connected one after the other.
(n.) A book, television, or radio program which consists of several episodes.
(n.) A group of matches between two sides.
(adj.) Connected one after the other in a circuit.

Draft

(n.) An early version of a written work (such as a book, essay, etc.).
(n.) A current of air, usually coming into a room or vehicle.
(n.) An order for money to be paid.
(n.) The system of forcing people to serve in the military; conscription.

Contend

(v.) To strive in opposition; to contest; to dispute.
(v.) To struggle or exert oneself to get or keep something.

Focus On: Vocabulary

B) Fill in the blanks with the correct word from this unit's words, make necessary structural changes to the word, then write the correct definition of the word being used on the line below the sentence.

1) My uncle immigrated to Canada to avoid the _____.
_____

2) The Mets are playing the Yankees in the famous subway _____.
_____

3) When the boss came, the employees _____ to the conference room.
_____

4) They _____ martial arts moves into their dance performance.
_____

5) A(n) _____ of events led to the failure of the organization.
_____

6) The competitors _____ against each other for first place in the competition.
_____

7) "Harry Potter" is an all-time favorite book _____.
_____

8) Tonight's homework is to revise the first _____ of our essays.
_____

9) Geese _____ from Canada to Florida and back again.
_____

10) Many Mongoloid groups _____ south after crossing the Bering land bridge.
_____

11) Payment must be made by bank _____ drawn on banks in most countries.
_____

12) The Joneses _____ that the right to the land is ancestrally theirs.
_____

13) Children with mild learning difficulties are _____ into certain classes at some schools.
_____

14) The programmers are _____ all of the new code to the back-up server.
_____

15) The asylum seekers are well _____ into communities around America.
_____

16) A(n) _____ coming from that window is chilling my whole room.
_____

17) Christmas lights must be connected in a(n) _____ for them to work properly.
_____

54

C) Choose the correct definition from the word list page, then write it under the given paragraphs.

1) We will **contend** against these troubles by trying to persuade the respectable classes of society to the banishment of alcoholic beverages. You who move in elegant and refined associations; you who drink the best liquors; you who never drink until you lose your balance: consider that you have in your power the redemption of this land from drunkenness. Empty your cellars and wine-closets of the beverage, and then come out and give us your hand, your vote, your prayers, your sympathies.

_____

_____

_____

2) Heavy imports are always a potent factor in raising the level of exchange rates. Under whatever financial arrangement or from whatever point merchandise is imported into the United States, payment is almost invariably made by **draft** on London, Paris, or Berlin. At times when imports run especially heavy, demand from importers for exchange often outweighs every other consideration, forcing rates up to high levels.

_____

_____

_____

3) The Great Spirit brought the Alabama Indians from the ground between the Cahawba and Alabama rivers, and they believe that they are the right possessors of this soil. The Muscogees formerly called themselves Alabamians, but other tribes called them Oke-choy-atte. The earliest oral tradition of the Alibamu migration is that they **migrated** from the Cahawba and Alabama rivers to the junction of the Tuscaloosa and Coosa rivers.

_____

_____

_____

4) Michelson sought to place the phenomenon of electronic texts within the context of broader trends within information technology and scholarly communication. She argued that electronic texts are of most use to researchers to the extent that the researchers' working context (i.e., their relevant bibliographic sources, collegial feedback, analytic tools, notes, drafts, etc.), along with their field's primary and secondary sources, also is accessible in electronic form and can be **integrated** in ways that are unique to the online environment.

_____

_____

_____

5) The world learned a lesson when the Boxer Rebellion broke out in China. For the Chinese Government was perhaps the oldest in the world and the Chinese nation the most numerous. The revolt grew out of a **series** of aggressions by certain European powers, especially Great Britain, Germany, France, and Russia, that claimed important positions and valuable pieces of territory in China. Because of the fact that China had lost her vision, and had not even been stimulated to realizing facts by the example of Japan, China was at this time an incoherent aggregation of 320 separate states.

_____

_____

_____

Unit 18:
Technique - Constrain - Generate - Abstract - Assert

A) Know the definitions - Read through each definition and get a feeling for the meaning of each. If you choose to, memorize the words as explained in "Mesmerizing Memorization Method".

Technique

(n.) The practical aspects of a given art, occupation etc.; formal requirements.
(n.) Practical ability in some given field or practice, often as opposed to creativity or imaginative skill.
(n.) A method of achieving something or carrying something out, especially one requiring some skill or knowledge.

Constrain

(v.) To force by restricting, or limiting.
(v.) To keep within close bounds; to confine.
(v.) To reduce a result in response to limited resources.

Generate

(v.) To bring into being; give rise to.
(v.) To produce as a result of a chemical or physical process.
(v.) To procreate, beget; to give birth to.
(v.) To appear or occur.

Abstract

(n.) An abridgment or summary of a longer publication.
(n.) The theoretical way of looking at things; something that exists only in idealized form.
(n.) A summary title of the key points detailing a tract of land, for ownership; abstract of title.
(adj.) Pertaining to the formal aspect of art, such as the lines, colors, shapes, and the relationships among them.

Assert

(v.) To say with force or confidence.
(v.) To use or exercise and thereby prove the existence of.
(v.) To maintain or defend, as a cause or a claim.

Focus On: Vocabulary

B) Fill in the blanks with the correct word from this unit's words, make necessary structural changes to the word, then write the correct definition of the word being used on the line below the sentence.

1) Group discussions _____ many new ideas to improve our products.
_____

2) Our organization will _____ resources while maintaining quality to decrease expenses.
_____

3) Paul Jackson Pollock is known as one of the most famous _____ expressionism painters.
_____

4) Our company uses solar driven chemistry to _____ hydrogen from water.
_____

5) The scientist _____ to his colleagues that his experiment was a success.
_____

6) His _____ in flipping burgers keeps the juices inside and improves the taste.
_____

7) The professor required _____ of all the students' dissertations.
_____

8) We must _____ our rights and liberties if we wish to keep them.
_____

9) The police can't do their job because they are _____ by regulations.
_____

10) The musician seemingly _____ such happiness among the audience.
_____

11) Applying a few photo processing _____ can improve a photo's clarity.
_____

12) The Principal _____ his authority over the educational reforms.
_____

13) Call the county recorder to get the _____ for that property you own on Main Street.
_____

14) Early human ancestors _____ many offspring, but few survived.
_____

15) His arm must be _____ of all movement during the healing process.
_____

16) This new _____ of artificially growing organs is very controversial.
_____

17) Love and beauty are _____ concepts.
_____

C) Choose the correct definition from the word list page, then write it under the given paragraphs.

1) My readers will understand with what great regret why I took my pen and wrote the resignation to my office. Especially when I recall to mind my having been twice suspended from my duties for the efforts I had made in bringing about the changes which I have above referred to. And that at last, when I was no longer able to do my work, I was **constrained** to sever my connection with the Board who had come to look upon me as one actuated by a sense of duty.

_____

_____

2) The practice of heating rooms with portable gas or oil stoves with no provision for removing the products of combustion is lethal since the carbon dioxide is **generated** in sufficient quantities to render the air unfit for breathing. Rooms so heated also become very damp from the large amount of water vapor formed in the combustion, and which in cold weather condenses on the window glass, causing the glass to "sweat." Both coal and wood contain a certain amount of mineral substances which constitute the ashes.

_____

_____

3) The price at which I am holding the building is $200,000. If the buyer prefers not to assume the mortgage of $100,000, I think I can get the mortgagee to agree to accept payment for the note that he holds against me unless the buyer agrees to pay the unpaid taxes for last year and the assessments levied for improvements already made, I will not consider a sale. After all preliminary arrangements are made if you will prepare a contract of sale and forward it to me, I will have the **abstract** brought down to date and secured by a guaranty policy.

_____

_____

4) My desire has been to write a book that would be of some practical use, at least practically suggestive to the writer of fiction; therefore, the only natural way to approach **technique** has been adopted, and I have indulged in analysis only when the analysis would be useful in itself or would serve to clear away misconception. In other words, the book has been written strictly for the writer, not the reader of fiction, and that implies much.

_____

_____

5) It is stated that practical experience with gas mantles made of artificial silk—that is, silk made from wood pulp—has proved them to be far superior to those made of cotton, especially where the mantles are exposed to excessive vibration. Several German towns are said to be obtaining exceptionally good results from these new mantles used in conjunction with pressure gas, and it is **asserted** that the mantles are in good condition after being used for seven or eight weeks.

_____

_____

Unit 19:
Recovery - Transform - Correspond - Statistic - Element

A) Know the definitions - Read through each definition and get a feeling for the meaning of each. If you choose to, memorize the words as explained in "Mesmerizing Memorization Method".

Recovery

(n.) The act or process of regaining or repossession of something lost or stolen.
(n.) A return to normal health.
(n.) A return to former status or position.
(n.) Renewed growth after an economic slowdown.

Transform

(v.) To change greatly the appearance or form of.
(v.) To change the nature, condition or function of; to change in nature, disposition, heart, character, etc.

Correspond

(v.) To be equivalent or similar in character, quantity, quality, origin, structure, function etc.
(v.) To exchange messages, especially by postal letter, over a period of time.

Statistic

(n.) A single item in a statistical (understanding data) study.
(n.) A person, or personal event, reduced to being an item of statistical information.

Element

(n.) One of the simplest or essential parts or principles of which anything is made up of.
(n.) A small part of the whole.
(n.) Weather forces such as strong winds and rains.
(n.) A place or state of being that an individual or object is best suited to.
(n.) A group of people within a larger group having a particular common characteristic.
(n.) Each of more than one hundred substances that cannot be chemically interconverted or broken down into simpler substances and are primary constituents of matter.

Focus On: Vocabulary

B) Fill in the blanks with the correct word from this unit's words, make necessary structural changes to the word, then write the correct definition of the word being used on the line below the sentence.

1) The periodic table of elements has most of the _____ on earth, but more are in the universe.
_____

2) The New York Stock Exchange made an unbelievable _____ before the closing bell rang.
_____

3) The ancient device was exposed to the _____, yet still was undamaged.
_____

4) I am offering a reward for the _____ of my stolen ipad.
_____

5) I've been _____ with my pen pal in Japan for three years.
_____

6) The ground is a(n)_____ of the picture that is rarely considered as a major part.
_____

7) Many alchemists attempted to _____ lead into gold.
_____

8) The authorities are always investigating the criminal _____ in society.
_____

9) One can only _____ one's life by renewing the mind.
_____

10) The reason you're in debt is because your expenses do not _____ to your income.
_____

11) Bix survived the round after two knockdowns, then made a(n) _____ in the fifth round.
_____

12) The _____ on obesity costing the U.S. $ 147 billion a year is staggering.
_____

13) Numbers are the _____ of mathematics.
_____

14) He became just another _____ by dying from an overdose.
_____

15) If you put him in a social situation, he'll be in his _____.
_____

16) Doctors expect him to make a full _____.
_____

C) Choose the correct definition from the word list page, then write it under the given paragraphs.

1) I had a simple school form prepared and printed for the schools to report flu instances, copies of which were sent to the offices of the Governors of various states. Returns were made from a large number of schools, but as no information has been received from many more, I assume the schools' **statistic** on the flu cannot be acquired without having a representative journey to the schools to get the necessary information.

_____

_____

_____

2) For years he had been a failure in life. Everything he had tried had somehow fallen far below his expectations. Indeed, at the very time he was writing the Midwinter letters he was tramping the streets, going from newspaper office to office in New Orleans seeking work. Let us see now how these things in the life of Hearn **correspond** with the description of Ozias Midwinter: "From first to last the man's real character shrank back with a savage shyness from the rector's touch."

_____

_____

_____

3) Suddenly the scene was **transformed** for him back almost a score of years into the past. For, as Tommy pumped away, Miss Phœbe struck a low bass note on the organ and held it to test the volume of air that it contained. The church ceased to exist, so far as Father Abram was concerned. The deep, booming vibration that shook the little frame building was no note from an organ, but the humming of the mill machinery.

_____

_____

_____

4) Eight-tenths of the mortality amongst the aborigines of that region arises through intemperance, bringing on pulmonary disorders, pleurisy, pneumonia, disorders of the chest, consumption, etc., which carries them off to death so speedily that the ablest medical treatment seldom saves them. I may safely state that when their respiratory organs are once affected, **recovery** becomes hopeless. I have witnessed this so invariably within the last 10 years, as to look forward for death as soon as they are afflicted in the chest.

_____

_____

_____

5) Interaction between incidents and characters, arising from the unity of the whole conception, is the first essential **element** of a plot. The second essential element—and there are but two—is that the several incidents of the story possess climactic value, not necessarily climactic value in the sense of ascending tensity—though that is most desirable—but climactic value in that each event should have influence in forwarding the story to a definite end, that state of quiescence which is not attainable in real life short of the grave, but which fiction must postulate.

_____

_____

_____

Focus On: Vocabulary

Unit 20:
Estate - Investigate - Relative - Logic - Conduct

A) **Know the definitions** - Read through each definition and get a feeling for the meaning of each. If you choose to, memorize the words as explained in "Mesmerizing Memorization Method".

Estate

(n.) The collective property and liabilities of someone, especially a deceased person.
(n.) A large area of land, under single ownership.
(n.) A major social class or order of persons regarded collectively as part of the body politic of the country and formerly possessing distinct political rights.

Investigate

(v.) To inquire into or study in order to ascertain facts or information; research.
(v.) To examine, look into, or scrutinize in order to discover something hidden or secret.
(v.) To conduct an inquiry or examination.

Relative

(adj.) Connected to or depending on something else; comparative.
(adj.) Relevant; pertinent; related in some way.
(n.) Someone in the same family; someone connected by blood, marriage, or adoption.

Logic

(n.) A method of human thought that involves thinking in a step-by-step manner about solving a problem.
(n.) The study of the principles and criteria of valid inference (steps in reasoning, moving from premises to logical consequences.) and demonstration (showing that the inference works).
(n.) Any system of thought a particular person has.

Conduct

(v.) To lead; to direct; to manage.
(v.) To behave.
(v.) To serve as a medium for conveying; to transmit (heat, light, electricity, etc.).
(v.) To direct, as the leader in the performance of a musical composition.
(v.) To carry out (something organized).

Focus On: Vocabulary

B) Fill in the blanks with the correct word from this unit's words, make necessary structural changes to the word, then write the correct definition of the word being used on the line below the sentence.

1) The former governor retired and lived in _____ isolation on his estate.
_____

2) My son _____ himself well at the family get together.
_____

3) We _____ the matter from several different angles before deciding on an action.
_____

4) Philosophers state there are three branches of _____: deductive, inductive, and abductive.
_____

5) The general _____ thousands of troops in the great war.
_____

6) Private investigators _____ crimes to keep information out of the public eye.
_____

7) The three _____ of feudal lords, clergy and royal officers advised Kings on state matters.
_____

8) Carlos Kleiber, is said to have _____ his orchestras with much vigor.
_____

9) _____ to your earlier point on politics, I think citizens must choose their politicians carefully.
_____

10) The process of the scientific method involves making hypotheses based on _____.
_____

11) Ghost hunters were called in to _____ the causes of supernatural phenomena.
_____

12) My _____ always talk about the two dinner table taboos: politics and religion.
_____

13) This new metal _____ electricity and doesn't rust in water.
_____

14) After their father passed, they sold his entire _____, keeping nothing for themselves.
_____

15) The project manager tasked me to _____ experiments based on the new data.
_____

16) George Washington's _____ is situated on the banks of the Potomac River.
_____

17) No one can figure out his system of _____.
_____

C) Choose the correct definition from the word list page, then write it under the given paragraphs.

1) This primitive method of place specification deals only with places on the surface of rigid bodies and is dependent on the existence of points on this surface which are distinguishable from each other. But we can free ourselves from both of these limitations without altering the nature of our specification of position. If, for instance, a cloud is hovering over Times Square, then we can determine its position **relative** to the surface of the earth by erecting a pole perpendicularly on the Square, so that it reaches the cloud.

_____

_____

_____

2) Napoleon was swayed by the impulse of the age. He thought of nothing but representative governments. Often has he said to me, "I should like the era of representative governments to be dated from my time." His **conduct** in Italy and his proclamations ought to give, and in fact do give, weight to this account of his opinion. But there is no doubt that this idea was more connected with lofty views of ambition than a sincere desire for the benefit of the human race.

_____

_____

_____

3) He **investigated** the case with great care, for Dr. Roylott's conduct had long been notorious in the county, but he was unable to find any satisfactory cause of death. My evidence showed that the door had been fastened upon the inner side, and the windows were blocked by old-fashioned shutters with broad iron bars, which were secured every night. The chimney is wide but is barred up by four large staples. It is certain, therefore, that my aunt was quite alone when she met her end.

_____

_____

_____

4) And so you think, do you, that the chief use of **logic**, in real life, is to deduce conclusions from workable premises, and to satisfy yourself that the conclusions, deduced by other people, are correct? I only wish it were! Society would be much less liable to panics and other delusions, and political life, especially, would be a totally different thing, if even a majority of the arguments, that scattered broadcast over the world, were correct!

_____

_____

_____

5) Madame de Beauseant's **estate** was close to a little town in one of the most picturesque spots in the valley of the Auge. Here she and her husband raised barriers between themselves and social gatherings, barriers which no creature could overleap, and here the happy days of Switzerland were lived over again. For nine whole years, they knew happiness which it serves no purpose to describe.

_____

_____

_____

Unit 16-20 Review

Match the correct definition with the correct word by writing the correct definition' letter in the blank next to the word that corresponds to that definition.

_____1. Objective   A. The theoretical way of looking at things;

_____2. Element   B. To maintain or defend, as a cause or a claim

_____3. Conduct   C. Renewed growth after an economic slowdown.

_____4. Draft   D. To carry out

_____5. Relative   E. To overlook from a height

_____6. Recovery   F. To include as a constituent part or functionality.

_____7. Assert   G. Connected to or depending on something else

_____8. Abstract   H. A group of people within a larger group having a particular common characteristic.

_____9. Integrate   I. An order for money to be paid

_____10. Dominate   J. Not influenced by personal feelings or opinions in considering and representing facts.

Fill in the blanks with the correct word from this unit's words:

Panic struck Joanne; it was her first time being the lead detective, and she hadn't the slightest clue on how to _____ the DNA analysis team into the police department for this case. Previous attempts had led to a hostile work _____, the dissolution of the combined team, and an unsolved case. Vincent, another detective, broke the silence. "Your silence shows that maybe you aren't cut out for this, Jo", he said snidely. Joanne struggled within herself. _Are you going to let him talk to you like that in front of everyone, Joanne? No way!_ With piercing eye contact, her demeanor _____. "There's no need to speak to me that way, Vincent. I was organizing my thoughts on how to start _____ ideas. Now team, how shall we proceed with _____ this crime?"

Unit 21:
Reproach - Fiscal - Subsequent - Avenue - Index

A) Know the definitions - Read through each definition and get a feeling for the meaning of each. If you choose to, memorize the words as explained in "Mesmerizing Memorization Method".

Reproach

(v.) To criticize someone.
(v.) To disgrace, or bring shame upon someone.
(n.) A mild rebuke, or an implied criticism.

Fiscal

(adj.) Related to the treasury of a country, company, region or city, particularly to govt. spending and earnings.
(adj.) Pertaining to finance and money in general; financial.

Subsequent

(adj.) Following in time; coming or being after something else at any time.
(adj.) Following in order of place; succeeding.

Avenue

(n.) A broad street, especially one bordered by trees.
(n.) A channel, contact, or a means to communicate.
(n.) A method or means by which something may be accomplished.

Index

(n.) An alphabetical listing of items and their location.
(n.) The index finger; the forefinger.
(n.) That which points out; that which shows, indicates, manifests, or discloses.
(n.) A listing of companies in financial markets, stock and bond market.
(v.) To arrange an index for something, especially a long text.
(v.) To inventory; to take stock.

Focus On: Vocabulary

B) Fill in the blanks with the correct word from this unit's words, make necessary structural changes to the word, then write the correct definition of the word being used on the line below the sentence.

1) The President ran his second campaign as a(n) _____ conservative.
_____

2) The _____ of a book lists words or phrases and the pages where they can be found.
_____

3) We submitted reports through official _____, but received no responses.
_____

4) The new clerk is _____ all of the company's supplies.
_____

5) The economy flourished in the _____ years after the small depression.
_____

6) Our computer _____ millions of new records every second.
_____

7) The officer's conduct had always been beyond even_____ in all of his duties.
_____

8) Our team approached the problem by several _____, but none worked.
_____

9) Most people cannot use their _____ finger as well as their other fingers.
_____

10) My sister _____ anyone who annoys her while she's reading.
_____

11) As we drove up the _____ birds flew by our car.
_____

12) The government must adopt a strict _____ policy to avoid an national economic crisis.
_____

13) Test results serve as a(n) _____ of the teacher's effectiveness at teaching.
_____

14) By lying about the funds, the politician _____ herself.
_____

15) The consequences of the main character's mistakes will be discussed in _____ chapters.
_____

16) The S&P 500 is a US stock market _____ based on of 500 large companies.
_____

C) Choose the correct definition from the word list page, then write it under the given paragraphs.

1) I do not for a moment suppose that Universal Free Trade—even if the adoption of such a policy were conceivable—would inaugurate an era of universal and permanent peace. Whatever **fiscal** policy be adopted by the great commercial nations of the world, it is wholly illusory to suppose that the risk of war can be altogether avoided in the future. But I am equally certain that Free Trade, by mutually enlisting a number of influential material interests in the cause of peace, tends to ameliorate peaceful relations and thus diminishes the probability of war.

_____

_____

_____

2) He **reproached** his wife with her inattention and her habitual neglect of the children. If it was not a mother's place to look after children, whose on earth was it? He himself had his hands full with his brokerage business. He could not be in two places at once; making a living for his family on the street, and staying at home to see that no harm befell them. He talked in a monotonous, insistent way.

_____

_____

_____

3) The plan of the buildings for Washington D.C. was drawn by a Frenchman named L'Enfant. The ground, marked out for them, was fourteen miles in circumference. The streets run north and south, east and west, but to prevent that sameness which would result from their all crossing each other at right angles, several **avenues** have been laid out, in different parts of the city, which run transversely.

_____

_____

_____

_____

4) On a daily basis, it is not uncommon for traders, be they hedge fund managers or the average day trader to refer to several sources to plan their trades. Though many traders have their specific strategies and resources, others view several sector **indexes** to see if they're bullish or bearish, rising or falling, then choosing individual stocks to place their trade on.

_____

_____

_____

5) It is obvious that the discovery of new tribes, and the first account of manners formerly unknown, are by no means more interesting than the **subsequent** history of those tribes, and the changes which rapidly take place in their manners. The greatest obligations of those adventurous people who visited these islands is to give such statements of what they saw. These would enable us to trace the progress of society in one of its earliest stages and to estimate the effects produced by the sudden change in their circumstances which the natives have experienced from their meetings with Europeans.

_____

_____

_____

Unit 22:
Saunter - Plausible - Summary - Yield - Brief

A) Know the definitions - Read through each definition and get a feeling for the meaning of each. If you choose to, memorize the words as explained in "Mesmerizing Memorization Method".

Saunter

(v.) To stroll, or walk at a leisurely pace.

Plausible

(adj.) Seemingly or apparently valid, likely, or acceptable.
(adj.) Receiving approval, specifically pleasing; seemingly well-reasoned.

Summary

(n.) Concise; brief or presented in a condensed form; a shortened form of.
(n.) Performed speedily and without formal ceremony.
(n.) A short writing about the main points.

Yield

(v.) To bear or bring forth a natural product as foods such as fruits or vegetables, places that give food.
(v.) To give way; to allow another to pass first.
(v.) To surrender, relinquish or capitulate.
(v.) To produce as a result in mathematics.
(n.) Profit earned from an investment; return on investment.

Brief

(adj.) Of short duration; happening quickly.
(adj.) Concise; taking few words.
(adj.) Occupying a small distance, area or spatial extent; short.
(n.) A summary of a client's court case written by an attorney for use in conducting a case.
(n.) Undershorts; tight underpants.

Focus On: Vocabulary

B) Fill in the blanks with the correct word from this unit's words, make necessary structural changes to the word, then write the correct definition of the word being used on the line below the sentence.

1) The queen's reign was _____ but filled with many history-making events.
_____

2) The expected _____ of our various investments will be greater than any other year.
_____

3) We _____ under the trees and through the fields all day long without a care in the world.
_____

4) The valedictorian's acceptance speech was _____, but to the point.
_____

5) The cashier gave a(n) _____ excuse to the manager for being late.
_____

6) When driving a car, always _____ the right of way to pedestrians.
_____

7) _____ executions broke the resistance of the rebels.
_____

8) I listened to the _____ speaker as he addressed his arguments to the assembly.
_____

9) I wear boxers most of the time but when I play soccer, I always wear _____.
_____

10) Our orchards _____ the juiciest fruit you can imagine.
_____

11) Most of the guys wore surfer shorts on the beach, but Jet wore _____ trunks.
_____

12) The students wrote _____ of the magazine articles for their English class.
_____

13) 6 + 6 _____ 12.
_____

14) The lawyer prepared a(n) _____ to present to the judge on behalf of his client.
_____

15) This _____ review reflects the major areas discussed at the convention.
_____

16) The last battalion of defenders refuses to _____ to the invading enemy.
_____

C) Choose the correct definition from the word list page, then write it under the given paragraphs.

1) The secretaries' duties were ambiguous. She overlooked the books that Scraggs kept and sent out the bills. She kept the key to the cash box and had charge of the safe. She made the entries in the docket and performed most of the duties of a regular managing clerk. She had been admitted to the bar. She checked up the charge accounts and on Saturdays paid off the office force. In addition to all these things she occasionally took a hand at a **brief**, drew most of the pleadings, and kept track of everything that was done in the various cases.

_____

_____

_____

2) The earth, by great and secondary tides, speaks to the planets, her sisters. Do they reply to her? We must think so. From their fluid elements, they also must rise, sensible to the rise of the waters of the earth. The mutual attraction, the tendency of each star to emerge from egotism, must cause sublime dialogues to be heard in the skies. Unfortunately, the human ear can hear but the least part of them. There is another point to be considered. It is not at the very moment of the passing of the influential planet that the sea **yields** to its influence. She is in no such servile haste to obey; she must have time to feel and obey the attraction. She has to call the idle waters to herself.

_____

_____

_____

3) The prattle of children may be grateful music to our ears when we are in one mood, and excruciatingly discordant noise when we are in another. What appeals to us as a good practical joke one day, may seem a piece of unwarranted impertinence on another. A proposition which looks entirely **plausible** under the hopeful mood induced by a persuasive orator may appear wholly untenable a few hours later.

_____

_____

_____

4) In July or August, soon after the swarming season is over, the bees expel the drones from the hive. They sometimes sting them, and sometimes gnaw the roots of their wings, so that when driven from the hive, they cannot return. If not treated in either of these **summary** ways, they are so persecuted and starved, that they soon perish. The hatred of the bees extends even to the young which are still unhatched: they are mercilessly pulled from the cells, and destroyed with the rest.

_____

_____

_____

5) The woods around the town of Styles were very beautiful. After the walk across the open park, it was pleasant to **saunter** lazily through the cool glades. There was hardly a breath of wind, the very chirp of the birds was faint and subdued. I strolled on a little way, and finally flung myself down at the foot of a grand old beech-tree. My thoughts of mankind were kindly and charitable. I even forgave Poirot for his absurd secrecy. In fact, I was at peace with the world.

_____

_____

_____

Unit 23:
Emerge - Presume - Impose - Pursue - Conflict

A) Know the definitions - Read through each definition and get a feeling for the meaning of each. If you choose to, memorize the words as explained in "Mesmerizing Memorization Method".

Emerge

(v.) To come into view.
(v.) To come out of a situation, object or a liquid.
(v.) To become known.

Presume

(v.) To perform, do (something) without authority; to lay claim to without permission.
(v.) To assume or suggest to be true (without proof); to take for granted.

Impose

(v.) To establish or apply by authority.
(v.) To be an inconvenience (on or upon).
(v.) To enforce: compel to behave in a certain way.

Pursue

(v.) To follow urgently, originally with intent to capture or harm; to chase.
(v.) To aim for, go after.
(v.) To participate in (an activity, business etc.); to practice, follow.

Conflict

(n.) A clash or disagreement, often violent, between two or more opposing groups or individual.
(n.) An incompatibility, as of two things that cannot be simultaneously fulfilled.
(v.) To be at odds (with); to disagree or be incompatible.
(v.) To overlap (with), as in a schedule.

Focus On: Vocabulary

B) Fill in the blanks with the correct word from this unit's words, make necessary structural changes to the word, then write the correct definition of the word being used on the line below the sentence.

1) My nephew plans to _____ a career in local politics.
_____

2) You are my boss and I wouldn't _____ to tell you how to do your job.
_____

3) The hikers, lost for two weeks, _____ from the mountains to emergency workers.
_____

4) I wanted to attend the meeting but there's a(n) _____ in my schedule that day.
_____

5) The _____ between the government and the rebels began three years ago.
_____

6) I _____ her to be his sister, but they were actually strangers.
_____

7) A leader who _____ his decisions on his citizens becomes a tyrant.
_____

8) The truth _____ after many accusations had been alleged about the President.
_____

9) The police _____ any criminal caught in the act of committing a crime.
_____

10) If you _____ yourself on others, then you might become disliked.
_____

11) The ocean _____ from the street as we drove towards it.
_____

12) Let's make sure our schedules don't _____ with one another's.
_____

13) The UN _____ peace as its first action between nations involved in a conflict.
_____

14) Everyone hates our new group leader because she _____ her will on the rest of us.
_____

15) Because of his inability to compromise, he _____ with most politicians.
_____

Focus On: Vocabulary

C) For this section, choose the correct definition from the definition page, write it on the lines under each paragraph.

1) The works of Charles F. Lummis will never be forgotten—*The Land of Poco Tiempo*; *Mesa, Canyon and Pueblo*. Adolph Bandelier, another writer, and Lummis were very good friends and although their opinions and ideas **conflicted** at times, this friendship was never broken. Many times has Lummis visited Frijoles and many times has he stayed in the old Indian cave rooms, even in quite recent times, when other accommodations were available.

_____
_____
_____
_____

2) I spent that day mostly in the woods, having the alternative before me,—to go home and be whipped to death, or stay in the woods and be starved to death. That night, I fell in with Sandy Jenkins, a slave with whom I was somewhat acquainted. Sandy had a free wife who lived about four miles from Mr. Covey's; and it being Saturday, he was on his way to see her. I told him my circumstances, and he very kindly invited me to go home with him. I went home with him, and talked this whole matter over, and got his advice as to what course it was best for me to **pursue**. I found Sandy an old adviser.

_____
_____
_____
_____

3) Standing upright on a rock, irritated and menacing, Professor Hardwigg, like the ferocious Ajax, seemed to defy the fates. I, however, took upon myself to interfere and to **impose** some sort of check upon such foolish enthusiasm. "Listen to me, Uncle," I said, in a firm but temperate tone of voice, "there must be some limit to ambition here below. It is utterly useless to struggle against the impossible. We are utterly unprepared for a sea voyage; it is simply madness.

_____
_____
_____
_____

4) We took our time, and we searched everywhere. I have had long experience in these affairs. I took the entire building, room by room; devoting the nights of a whole week to each. We examined, first, the furniture of each apartment. We opened every possible drawer; and I **presume** you know that, to a properly trained police agent, such a thing as a secret drawer is impossible. Any man is a dolt who permits a 'secret' drawer to escape him in a search of this kind. The thing is so plain.

_____
_____
_____
_____

5) Only a half-mile away is the Stone Lions Shrine. Carved out of native tuff are the life-size images of two mountain lions and around them is an enclosure—a low wall of blocks of volcanic tuff. It is said that even the Zuñi Indians made pilgrimages to this shrine because they believed this to be the entrance to Shipapolima, the underworld from which their ancestors **emerged**.

_____
_____
_____
_____

Unit 24:
Domain - Eloquent - Decree - Complex - Peculiar

A) Know the definitions - Read through each definition and get a feeling for the meaning of each. If you choose to, memorize the words as explained in "Mesmerizing Memorization Method".

Domain

(n.) A geographic area owned or controlled by a single person or organization.
(n.) A field or sphere of activity, influence, expertise or academics.
(n.) A group of related items, topics, or subjects.
(n.) Any DNS domain name used on the internet which translates into an IP address.
(n.) The highest rank in the classification of organisms, above kingdom.

Eloquent

(n.) Fluently persuasive and articulate; well-spoken.

Decree

(n.) An edict or law.
(n.) The judicial decision in a litigated cause rendered by a court of equity.
(v.) To command by a decree (by a law).

Complex

(adj.) Made up of multiple parts; composite.
(adj.) Not simple, easy, or straightforward; complicated.
(n.) A network of interconnected systems.
(n.) A collection of buildings with a common purpose, such as a university or apartments.
(n.) A psychological dislike or fear of a particular thing.

Peculiar

(adj.) Out of the ordinary; odd; strange; unusual.
(adj.) Common or usual for a certain place or circumstance; specific or particular.

Focus On: Vocabulary

B) Fill in the blanks with the correct word from this unit's words, make necessary structural changes to the word, then write the correct definition of the word being used on the line below the sentence.

1) The night sky lit up with a(n) _____ series of lights when the company's transformer blew.
_____

2) Ideas that are made up of several simple ones put together are called _____ ideas.
_____

3) The court _____ the restoration of our ancestral property.
_____

4) The vast _____ of epidemic diseases of mammals can be cured by antibiotics.
_____

5) Lemurs are _____ to Madagascar.
_____

6) Courts grant _____ of adoption to individuals who can provide for a child.
_____

7) The king ruled his _____ harshly.
_____

8) Our teacher tried to explain a(n) _____ theory in physics, but no one could understand it.
_____

9) All life is classified into: _____, kingdom, phylum, class, order, family, genus, and species.
_____

10) President Eisenhower warned the U.S. of the dangers of the military-industrial _____.
_____

11) Over the years great thinkers have added many topics into the _____ of philosophy.
_____

12) Buddy has a(n) _____ about working for anyone, so he's self-employed.
_____

13) The attendees were deeply impressed by the founders' _____ speech.
_____

14) Some families prefer to live in apartment _____ while others prefer houses.
_____

15) The king sent out a(n) _____ that all people of the realm will become citizens.
_____

16) Register a(n) _____ name, like "folpbooks.com" so you can create a company website.
_____

C) Choose the correct definition from the word list page, then write it under the given paragraphs.

1) There are no towers in the land more time-honored than my gloomy, gray, hereditary halls. Our line has been called a race of visionaries; and in many striking particulars—in the character of the family mansion—in the frescos of the chief saloon—in the tapestries of the dormitories—in the chiseling of some buttresses in the armory—but more especially in the gallery of antique paintings—in the fashion of the library chamber—and, lastly, in the very **peculiar** nature of the library's contents—there is more than sufficient evidence to warrant the belief.

_____

_____

_____

2) Wherever you go within the **complex**, the olfactory sense is tantalized by the numerous smells of its inhabitants cooking up countless meals. Whether you take a sniff on the first floor or open the door from the stairwell on the fifteenth to inhale, the smells of sauerkraut, marinara sauce, curry, or even tum yum soup can be smelled. Personally, I like the 7th floor best of all because when walking down the long and wide hallway, a symphony of what I imagine to be all the nations of the world's foods can be inhaled in one big whiff.

_____

_____

_____

3) So that my readers may have something besides the dull theory of needlework, which includes sewing, patching, mending, darning, stitching, embroidery, and much more, the work is enlivened by some useful patterns. Many of these patterns are new, others derived from the artistic productions of such countries and epochs as have become famous by special excellence in the **domain** of needlework. These countries near and far have unique ways in which they undertake the art of needlework and give us the pleasure of developing and fusing our skills.

_____

_____

_____

_____

4) Jurgis found himself in a large hall, elaborately decorated with flags and bunting; and after the chairman had made his little speech, and the orator of the evening rose up, amid an uproar from the band—only fancy the emotions of Jurgis upon making the discovery that the personage was none other than the famous and **eloquent** Senator Spareshanks, who had addressed the "Doyle Republican Association" at the stockyards, and helped to elect Mike Scully's.

_____

_____

_____

5) In the earlier days of the siege, there was no rationing of provisions, though the price of meat was fixed by government **decree**. At the end of September, however, the authorities decided to limit the supply to a maximum of 500 oxen and 4000 sheep per diem. It was also decided that the butchers' shops should only open on every fourth day when four days' meat should be distributed at the official prices.

_____

_____

_____

Unit 25:
Allocate - Ethnic - Option - Decline - Accurate

A) Know the definitions - Read through each definition and get a feeling for the meaning of each. If you choose to, memorize the words as explained in "Mesmerizing Memorization Method".

Allocate

(v.) To set aside for a purpose.
(v.) To distribute according to a plan.
(v.) To reserve a portion of memory for use by a computer program.

Ethnic

(adj.) Of or relating to a group of people having common racial, national, religious or cultural origins.
(adj.) Belonging to a foreign culture.

Option

(n.) One of a set of choices that can be made.
(n.) The freedom or right to choose.
(n.) A contract giving the holder the right to buy or sell an asset at a set strike price.

Decline

(v.) To move downwards, to fall, to drop.
(v.) To become weaker or worse.
(v.) To refuse.
(n.) A sloping downward.
(n.) A reduction or diminution of activity.

Accurate

(adj.) Giving a true or exact result.
(adj.) Deviating only slightly or within acceptable limits.

Focus On: Vocabulary

B) Fill in the blanks with the correct word from this unit's words, make necessary structural changes to the word, then write the correct definition of the word being used on the line below the sentence.

1) His health _____ every winter with the onset of each new flu season.
_____

2) You have the _____ to eat either healthy or unhealthily, but not both.
_____

3) As a family, we must decide to _____ funds for our summer vacations.
_____

4) A thermometer gives a(n) _____ measure of temperature.
_____

5) Management's refusal of the workers' demands resulted in a(n) _____ in productivity.
_____

6) The option writer sold the _____ to the option buyer through a contract.
_____

7) I'm sorry, I will have to _____ your generous offer.
_____

8) I like to eat _____ food.
_____

9) Most K–12 education funds are _____ for the cost of operating schools.
_____

10) Running down a hill's _____ is easier than up its incline.
_____

11) The program manager _____ memory to programs in a computer.
_____

12) The fortune tellers' predictions of events were surprisingly _____.
_____

13) There are many _____ Chinese in many countries in Asia.
_____

14) Parents should present _____ that direct their kids in a positive way.
_____

15) The dollar has _____ rapidly in the last two decades.
_____

C) Choose the correct definition from the word list page, then write it under the given paragraphs.

1) He did not stop to look back now, but urged his team to top speed with whip and voice: "*Musha! Arr-rr! Musha!*" Obediently the leader swung into an ice ravine. It was downhill, so the man threw himself on the sledge. His weight added to its momentum, and the dogs seemed not to touch the ground as they raced ahead, striving to keep the traces taut. The leader turned sharply to the left, and the man hung far out on the flying sledge to keep it from tipping. At a steep **decline** now, the hind feet of the nearest dogs were rattling on the curved runners, though they were doing their best.

_____

_____

_____

2) Richard was not so astonished at Barbara's coolness, or her courage, or the business-like way in which she tucked the great hoof under her arm, or even at the **accurate** aim which brought the right sort of blow down on the head of nail after nail in true line with its length to fasten shoe on the horse. But he was astonished at the strength of her little hand, the hardness of her muscles, covered with just fat enough to make form and movement alike beautiful, and the knowing skill with which she twisted off the ends of the nails: she was a natural.

_____

_____

_____

3) There are no natural and fixed limits to the territory. Its outline serves merely the purposes of convenience. For this reason, the peoples within the whole area are based, not upon natural ecological provinces such as mountain ranges, valleys, or river basins, but upon **ethnic** or "tribal" boundaries. Moreover, since there is no necessary interrelationship between these peoples, each is considered as a separate entity, and its population is recognized separately.

_____

_____

_____

4) The investors are a most intriguing group. Normative, law abiding, businessmen, who stumbled across methods to secure excessive yields on their capital and are looking to borrow their way into increasing it. By cleverly participating in bond tenders, by devising ingenious **option** strategies, or by arbitraging - yields of up to 300% can be collected in the immature markets of transition without the normally associated risks.

_____

_____

_____

5) Martha went about her work as usual, collecting the eggs and **allocating** them in their cardboard boxes, then setting off in the station wagon on her Tuesday morning run. She had expected a deluge of questions from her customers. She was not disappointed. "Is Terry really way up there all alone, Martha?" "Aren't you *scared*, Martha?" "I do hope they can get him back down all right, Martha." She supposed it must have given them quite a turn to have their egg woman change into a star mother overnight.

_____

_____

_____

Unit 21-25 Review

Match the correct definition with the correct word by writing the correct definition' letter in the blank next to the word that corresponds to that definition.

_____ 1. Presume   A. Seemingly or apparently valid, likely, or acceptable

_____ 2. Decree   B. To enforce; compel to behave in a certain way

_____ 3. Allocate   C. To criticize someone.

_____ 4. Domain   D. To stroll, or walk at a leisurely pace

_____ 5. Fiscal   E. To refuse

_____ 6. Saunter   F. An edict or law

_____ 7. Plausible   G. A group of related items, topics, or subjects.

_____ 8. Decline   H. To assume or suggest to be true

_____ 9. Impose   I. To distribute according to a plan

_____ 10. Reproach   J. Pertaining to finance and money in general

Fill in the blanks with the correct word from this unit's words:

_____ policy, more widely used after World War II, is one way the government of the United States influences the nation's economy. Fiscal policy is implemented by either a) adjusting the tax rate, or b) adjusting government spending. Monetary policy, another tool of government influence, _____ around the same time. These two policies are used in a mix, depending on the economic goals of the country. Influencing an entire economy, however, is a rather _____ task, and could _____ unfavorable results if the effects are not calculated properly. To avoid a _____ in economic growth, economists must carefully consider what to do to stimulate the economy through fiscal policy.

Unit 26:
Challenge - Definite - Obvious - Potent - Disdain

A) Know the definitions - Read through each definition and get a feeling for the meaning of each. If you choose to, memorize the words as explained in "Mesmerizing Memorization Method".

Challenge

(n.) A difficult task, especially one that is enjoyable because of that difficulty.
(n.) A confrontation; a dare.
(n.) An action meant to convince a person to perform an action they otherwise would not.
(n.) The act of appealing a ruling or decision of a court of administrative agency.
(v.) To invite someone to take part in a competition.
(v.) To dispute something.

Definite

(n.) Having distinct, or exact, limits.
(n.) Free from any doubt or uncertainty.
(n.) Determined; resolved.

Obvious

(adj.) Easily discovered, seen, or understood; self-explanatory.

Potent

(adj.) Possessing strength.
(adj.) Powerfully effective.
(adj.) Having a sharp or offensive taste and smell.
(adj.) Very powerful or effective in.

Disdain

(n.) The feeling or attitude of regarding someone or something as inferior or worthless.

Focus On: Vocabulary

B) Fill in the blanks with the correct word from this unit's words, make necessary structural changes to the word, then write the correct definition of the word being used on the line below the sentence.

1) The teacher set a(n) _____ for his students to improve their study habits.
_____

2) The American flag is a(n) _____ symbol of the freedom.
_____

3) The _____ he felt for his neighbor was obvious when he ignored him on the street.
_____

4) The lawyer's _____ to the court's decisions will take a long time to reverse.
_____

5) Some say there is no _____ truth outside of the natural sciences and math.
_____

6) I _____ the accuracy of this witness' statement since he wasn't at the scene.
_____

7) We've fixed a(n) _____ date for the next rally.
_____

8) Whatever you're boiling over there, it sure is _____ stuff.
_____

9) I enjoy mental _____ that make me think.
_____

10) The presidential candidate made _____ arguments that no one could refute.
_____

11) The _____ way of reducing trash is by recycling recyclable items.
_____

12) I _____ you to a game of… chess!
_____

13) He needed to take a(n) _____ medicine for his bacterial infection.
_____

14) His nephew posed a(n) _____ to the king's authority.
_____

15) _____ standards must be maintained for the pasteurization of milk.
_____

C) Choose the correct definition from the word list page, then write it under the given paragraphs.

1) "Well, I rather think that's all in the past," said Elmer. "If Matt does half he declares he means to do, it's going to be the biggest thing that ever happened for the boys of Fairfield and Cramerton. And something more, fellows. I just rather guess we'd better be brushing up all we know of the great American national game of baseball. For Matt says he and his team are going to **challenge** the Hickory Ridge scouts to a big game."

_____
_____
_____

2) Criminal identification by means of fingerprints is one of the most **potent** factors in obtaining the apprehension of fugitives who might otherwise escape arrest and continue their criminal activities indefinitely. This type of identification also makes possible an accurate determination of the number of previous arrests and convictions which, of course, results in the imposition of more equitable sentences by the judiciary, inasmuch as the individual who repeatedly violates the law finds it impossible to pose successfully as a first, or minor, offender.

_____
_____
_____

3) Still, were these emotions without prejudice to his own love for his mother, and without the slightest bitterness respecting her; and, least of all, there was no shallow **disdain** toward her of superior virtue. He too plainly saw, that not his mother had made his mother; but the Infinite Haughtiness had first fashioned her; and then the haughty world had further molded her; nor had a haughty Ritual omitted to finish her.

_____
_____
_____

4) But this, at least, is true: in proportion as the worker knows the meaning of the work that he does,—in proportion as he sees it in its largest relations to society and to life,—his work is no longer the drudgery of routine toil. It becomes instead an intelligent process directed toward a **definite** goal. It has acquired that touch of artistry which, so far as human testimony goes, is the only pure and uncontaminated source of human happiness.

_____
_____
_____

5) Men thought the world was flat until Columbus thought it to be round. The earlier thought was a belief held because men had not the energy or the courage to question what those about them accepted and taught, especially as it was suggested and seemingly confirmed by **obvious** sensible facts. The thought of Columbus was a reasoned conclusion.

_____
_____
_____

Unit 27:
Flourish - Grade - Transparent - Discriminate - Restrict

A) Know the definitions - Read through each definition and get a feeling for the meaning of each. If you choose to, memorize the words as explained in "Mesmerizing Memorization Method".

Flourish

(v.) To thrive or grow well.
(v.) To prosper or fare well.
(v.) To be in a period of greatest influence.
(v.) To make bold and sweeping, fanciful, or wanton movements, by way of ornament, parade, bravado, etc.

Grade

(n.) A rating.
(n.) The performance of an individual or group on an examination or test, expressed by a number, letter.
(n.) A degree or level of something; a position within a scale; a degree of quality.
(n.) A slope (up or down) of a roadway, other passage, or geographical feature.
(n.) A level of primary and secondary education.
(v.) To assign scores to the components of an academic test.

Transparent

(adj.) See-through, clear; having the property that light passes through it so it can be seen through.
(adj.) Open for all to know, thereby reducing the chance of corruption.

Discriminate

(v.) To tell the difference between things based on features; to make distinctions.
(v.) To make decisions based on prejudice, e.g., color, socio-economic class, etc.

Restrict

(v.) To restrain within boundaries; to limit; to confine
(v.) To prevent (someone) from doing something

Focus On: Vocabulary

B) Fill in the blanks with the correct word from this unit's words, make necessary structural changes to the word, then write the correct definition of the word being used on the line below the sentence.

1) The magician took off his hat with a(n) _____ to hide the bunny under his cape.
_____

2) Little Timmy is entering the first _____ this year.
_____

3) Windows are _____.
_____

4) The rules of the contest _____ the contestants from eating anything but hot dogs.
_____

5) Picasso's paintings termed *'Collage'* and *'Cubism'* _____ before WWI.
_____

6) This extremely fine- _____ coin is rare, so it is worth a pretty penny.
_____

7) Being colorblind, he was unable to _____ between the red and yellow sweaters.
_____

8) Only use food _____ plastic containers when pouring hot liquids for storing.
_____

9) Our crops are _____ in this season's warm weather.
_____

10) Topographic maps show the _____ of hills' elevations with contour lines.
_____

11) There are laws that prohibit _____ against people for almost any reason.
_____

12) The professor had his Teacher's Assistant _____ all of the examinations.
_____

13) The city _____ after implementing the Mayor's new reforms.
_____

14) The scientists _____ the test subjects to only the laboratories and dorms.
_____

15) All of the students in our math class received excellent _____ on the last test.
_____

16) We must conduct business in a(n) _____ way to prevent money mismanagement.
_____

C) Choose the correct definition from the word list page, then write it under the given paragraphs.

1) There is no system of numerically recording the general appearance and "look through" of a paper. The general character and tests of these papers correspond very closely with No. 1 machine-finish printing paper, according to the specifications of the U. S. Govt. Printing Office, which calls for a sheet not exceeding 0.0035 inch in thickness, free from unbleached or groundwood pulp, and ash not over 10 percent. The strength factor of such papers is about 0.28. These are the standards for general **grade** paper.

_____

_____

2) With the hopes of regaining the trust of the congregation, the religious organization's administrators have executed several changes. One of those changes has already been implemented due to the mismanagement of large sums of donations. This new policy will make all spending **transparent** to any one who wants to view the records. By doing this, the leaders hope to eliminate "misplaced" funds.

_____

_____

3) The teacher who does not permit and encourage diversity of operation in dealing with questions is imposing intellectual blinders upon pupils— **restricting** their vision to the one path the teacher's mind happens to approve. Probably the chief cause of devotion to rigidity of method is, however, that it seems to promise speedy, accurately measurable, correct results. The zeal for "answers" is the explanation of much of the zeal for rigid and mechanical methods. Forcing and overpressure have the same origin, and the same result upon alert and varied intellectual interest.

_____

_____

4) A savage tribe manages to live on a desert plain. It adapts itself. But its adaptation involves a maximum of accepting, tolerating, putting up with things as they are, and a minimum of active control. A civilized people enters upon the scene. It also adapts itself. It introduces irrigation; it searches the world for plants and animals that will **flourish** under such conditions; it improves, by careful selection, those which are growing there. As a consequence, the wilderness blossoms as a rose. The savage is merely habituated; the civilized man has habits which transform the environment.

_____

_____

5) When others are not doing what we would like them to or are threatening disobedience, we are most conscious of the need of controlling them. In such cases, our control becomes most direct, and at this point we are most likely to make the mistakes. We are even likely to take the influence of superior force for control, forgetting that while we may lead a horse to water we cannot make him drink; and that while we can shut a man up in a penitentiary we cannot make him penitent. In all such cases of immediate action upon others, we need to **discriminate** between physical results and moral results.

_____

_____

Unit 28:
Pinnacle - Lament - Comprehensive - Extract - Rational

A) Know the definitions - Read through each definition and get a feeling for the meaning of each. If you choose to, memorize the words as explained in "Mesmerizing Memorization Method".

Pinnacle

(n.) The highest point.
(n.) An all-time high; a point of greatest achievement or success.
(n.) A tall, sharp and craggy rock or mountain.
(n.) Vertical pyramidal or conical shaped structure at the top of buildings; a spire.

Lament

(v.) To express grief, suffering, or sadness.
(n.) A song expressing grief.

Comprehensive

(adj.) Broadly or completely covering; including a large proportion of something.

Extract

(n.) A portion of a book or document, used in another work; a citation; a quotation; an excerpt.
(n.) A decoction, solution, or infusion made by drawing out the essence of a substance to another.
(n.) A copy of writing; a certified copy of the proceedings in an action and the judgment of a court case.
(v.) To draw out; to pull out; to remove forcibly from a fixed position, as by traction or suction, etc.
(v.) To get something from someone who is unwilling to give.

Rational

(adj.) Capable of reasoning.
(adj.) Logically sound; not contradictory or otherwise absurd.
(adj.) Healthy or balanced intellectually; showing reasonableness.

B) Fill in the blanks with the correct word from this unit's words, make necessary structural changes to the word, then write the correct definition of the word being used on the line below the sentence.

1) His _____ statements drove his wife crazy.
_____

2) The dentist will need to _____ your rotten tooth from its socket.
_____

3) A hiker fell 40 ft from a rocky _____, but landed on a ledge which saved her life.
_____

4) The school _____ the death of its beloved music teacher.
_____

5) His fortune was at its _____ before he began to invest in the stock market.
_____

6) Aspirin is a(n) _____ of Willow Tree bark.
_____

7) This song is a(n) _____ for the deaths caused by communist regimes of the 20th century.
_____

8) _____ people do not treat others the way he treated us.
_____

9) I added a(n) _____ of a JRR Tolkien book in my essay about other worldly beings.
_____

10) Drug companies must do _____ research before submitting drugs to the FDA.
_____

11) The FBI agent _____ the information from the alleged terrorist.
_____

12) It is said that the builders of the pyramids of Giza painted the _____ with gold.
_____

13) Humans are _____ beings because we choose to follow a moral law.
_____

14) A printed copy of a certified _____ can be purchased at the clerk's office.
_____

15) The actor's _____ of fame was in his youth.
_____

Focus On: Vocabulary

C) Choose the correct definition from the word list page, then write it under the given paragraphs.

1) Bees sometimes act the part of highway robbers; some half dozen or more will waylay and attack a poor bee which is returning with a sack full of honey to his nest, like an honest trader, jogging home with a well-filled purse. They seize the poor bee and give him at once to understand that they must have the earnings of his industry. They do not slay him. Oh no! they are much too selfish to endanger their own precious persons; and even if they could kill him, without losing their weapons, they would still be unable to **extract** his sweets from the deep recesses of his honey bag: they, therefore, begin to bite and tease him, to eventually make him drop his load.

_____

_____

_____

2) The object of this work is to give the busy reader in acceptable form such a **comprehensive** knowledge as he would like to have, of the geography, history, picturesque attractions, peculiarities, productions and most salient features of our great country. The intention has been to make the book not only a work of reference, but a work of art and of interest as well, and it is burdened neither with too much statistics nor too intricate wordiness of description.

_____

_____

_____

3) The time study shows beyond argument the very quickest time in which a job can be done by an average man with the means at his disposal. If this is followed up by a **rational** organization, the Reward System will be entirely successful. But if an employer endeavors to foist the time study and Reward System on an existing rule-of-thumb organization, it will undoubtedly fail and will cause deep suspicion in the mind of the worker as well as being wholly unsatisfactory to the employer. It will be looked upon as an endeavor to get more out of the worker without an adequate return, and this, as a matter of fact, is just what it will be.

_____

_____

_____

4) I was very desirous to see the chief temple, and particularly the tower belonging to it, which is reckoned the highest in the kingdom. Accordingly, one day my nurse carried me there, but I may truly say I came back disappointed. The height is not above three thousand feet, reckoning from the ground to the **pinnacle** top; which, allowing for the difference between the size of those people and us in Europe, is no great matter for admiration.

_____

_____

_____

5) Much against my inclination, I was persuaded to leave Wuthering Heights and accompany her here. Little Hareton was nearly five years old, and I had just begun to teach him his letters. We made a sad parting, but Catherine's tears were more powerful than ours. When I refused to go, and when she found her entreaties did not move me, she went **lamenting** to her husband and brother.

_____

_____

_____

Unit 29:
Falter - Adapt - Demonstrate - Prescribe - Discord

A) Know the definitions - Read through each definition and get a feeling for the meaning of each. If you choose to, memorize the words as explained in "Mesmerizing Memorization Method".

Falter

(v.) To waver or be unsteady.
(v.) To speak in a weak and trembling manner; stammer.
(v.) To stumble, to walk in an unsteady way.
(v.) To lose faith or vigor; to doubt or abandon.
(v.) To hesitate in purpose or action.

Adapt

(v.) To make suitable; to make to correspond; to fit or suit.
(v.) To fit by alteration; to modify or remodel for a different purpose; to adjust.
(v.) To make changes to a book, play, poem, movie for it to be used in a different form.

Demonstrate

(v.) To show how to use.
(v.) To participate in or organize a demonstration (Negative or positive public display of opinion).

Prescribe

(v.) To order a drug, medical device, or method for use by a particular patient (under licensed authority).
(v.) To specify as a required procedure or ritual; to tell the way something must be done.

Discord

(n.) Lack of agreement or harmony.
(n.) Tension or violent conflict resulting from a lack of agreement; dissension.
(n.) An inharmonious or conflicting, combination of simultaneously sounded tones; a dissonance.

Focus On: Vocabulary

B) Fill in the blanks with the correct word from this unit's words, make necessary structural changes to the word, then write the correct definition of the word being used on the line below the sentence.

1) The protestors _____ outside of the chemical factory against their products.
_____

2) People should _____ themselves to any new situation.
_____

3) The doctor _____ rest and relaxation to the workaholic.
_____

4) After his initial success, he began to _____ when things became difficult.
_____

5) The programmer _____ how to use the newest version of the program.
_____

6) The coach saw the track star begin to _____ after he crossed the finish line.
_____

7) The regulations _____ that all students must wear uniforms on campus.
_____

8) After the war, _____ arose among the victors leading to another war.
_____

9) Although we had a major setback, we must not _____ in our resolve to win the election.
_____

10) The robotics specialist _____ an old drone between his robot's shoulders giving it sight.
_____

11) The composer used sounds of _____ to evoke war in his magnum opus.
_____

12) Her legs _____ while she presented her project in class.
_____

13) Shakespeare's *Hamlet* has been _____ numerous times into many books and films.
_____

14) Our two group's _____ originated from a misunderstanding.
_____

15) Her voice began to _____ in front of the large audience.
_____

C) Choose the correct definition from the word list page, then write it under the given paragraphs.

1) While the students lined up in front of Hong Ik University's main gate, others brought out signs, red bandanas, and banners. At exactly 9:15 AM, they began to **demonstrate** against the government's policies towards education reform. Within a few minutes, black vans pulled up to the side streets and out exited the riot police, ready to mollify the demonstrators, or attack them; whichever came first.

_____

_____

_____

2) We have done well, but we can do better. A thousand years shall not erase from the pages of history the part that we have played upon the American stage of action. Do not **falter** now, but rush to the help of the Justice Department with your banners floating in the breeze. We are said to be an unsolved problem. We are quoted as a vexatious question, and the eyes of the world are upon us. We can solve this problem, we can answer this question, and we can charm the gaze of the world.

_____

_____

_____

3) Today we depend for life's necessities almost wholly upon the activities of others. The work of thousands of human hands and thousands of human brains lies back of every meal you eat, every journey you take, every book you read, every telephone conversation, every telegram you receive, every garment you wear. **Adapt** or die is the way of nature. She has said with awful and inexorable finality that, whether you are a blade of grass on the Nevada desert or a man in the streets of London, you can win only as you adapt yourself to your environment. Only those who learn to adapt themselves to their fellows can win great or lasting rewards.

_____

_____

_____

4) Quevedo said: "Time passes, Señor Pedrarias, and with time, all flesh. Those who shall take our places follow close at our heels. A powerful rival converted into a firm ally is double compensation, and the father of four daughters has not the opportunity every day to refuse a governor for a son-in-law. Vasco Nuñez de Balboa, a man of no mean parts, well-born and famous, asks your daughter in marriage. Grant him his desire, and so heal **discord** and fortify your declining years."

_____

_____

_____

5) It is the universal testimony of those who have slept out-of-doors that the best-ventilated sleeping-room is far inferior in healthfulness to an outdoor sleeping-porch, open tent, or window tent (large enough to include the whole bed). For generations, outdoor sleeping has occasionally been used as a health measure in certain favorable climates and seasons. But only in the last two decades has it been used in ordinary climates and all the year round. Dr. Millet, a Brockton physician, began some years ago to **prescribe** outdoor sleeping for some shoe-factory workmen who were suffering from tuberculosis.

_____

_____

_____

Unit 30:
Uniform - Drone - Practitioner - Tentative - Foundation

A) Know the definitions - Read through each definition and get a feeling for the meaning of each. If you choose to, memorize the words as explained in "Mesmerizing Memorization Method".

Uniform

(adj.) Unvarying; all the same.
(adj.) Consistent; conforming to one standard.
(n.) A distinctive outfit (clothing) that serves to identify members of a group.

Drone

(n.) A male ant, bee or wasp, which does not work but can fertilize the queen bee.
(n.) One who performs menial or tedious work; a drudge.
(n.) A remotely controlled aircraft, an unmanned aerial vehicle (UAV).
(n.) A low-pitched hum or buzz.

Practitioner

(n.) A person who practices a profession or art, especially law or medicine.
(n.) One who does anything customarily or habitually.

Tentative

(adj.) Uncertain; subject to future change.
(adj.) Indicating a lack of confidence or certainty; hesitant.

Foundation

(n.) The act of founding, establishing or beginning to erect.
(n.) That upon which anything is founded; that on which anything stands, and by which it is supported. the lowest and supporting layer of a superstructure; underbuilding.
(n.) The result of the work to begin something; that which stabilizes and allows an enterprise or system to develop.
(n.) The element of a structure which connects it to the ground, and transfers loads from the structure to the ground.
(n.) A donation or legacy to support a charitable institution, and constituting a permanent fund.
(n.) Make-up that evens out skin tone, discolorations, and holes on the face.

Focus On: Vocabulary

B) Fill in the blanks with the correct word from the word list, make necessary structural changes to the word, then write the correct definition of the word being used on the line below the sentence.

1) The actress first applied primer, then _____ to her skin before adding the other make-up.
_____

2) The motivational speaker spoke in a low _____, boring the entire audience.
_____

3) We have _____ plans to meet tomorrow at noon.
_____

4) Almost all universities are _____ in their graduation ceremonies.
_____

5) The _____ of his institute brought him respect and wealth.
_____

6) I've been a(n) _____ of yoga for the last ten years.
_____

7) _____ are the ones that keep an ant colony thriving.
_____

8) The Bill and Melinda Gates Foundation is the largest private _____ in the U.S.
_____

9) Levittown's basic planning unit is rows of houses which are _____ in appearance.
_____

10) Inadequate _____ may cause buildings to subside, or worse, collapse.
_____

11) The young girl made _____ steps to the front of the classroom to give her speech.
_____

12) The _____ worker clocked in at 9 and out at 5 every day of the work week.
_____

13) The emergence of the information age transformed the _____ of the world.
_____

14) Most students around the world wear _____ to school.
_____

15) The President's policies laid a strong _____ for economic growth.
_____

16) A medical doctor is a legal _____ of medicine.
_____

17) The wedding planner hired a videographer with a(n) _____ for aerial shots of the wedding.
_____

C) Choose the correct definition from the word list page, then write it under the given paragraphs.

1) Light and soft, as though the wind were blowing the dust off the silver clouds that floated overhead, the first snow was falling over the barren lands. A lowland wind, which had already hardened and tightened the marshes, was blowing the snow skywards. The fine silvery dust, caught between the two air currents, danced lustily, blown here and there until it took hold of folds and rifts in the frozen land to meet other growing mountains of snow. The lowland wind, at first a mere breeze playfully teasing the north wind, like a child that kicks the bed-sheets before falling asleep, increased its force and swiftness with a steadily rising **drone** of the north wind. Then, a great calm followed.

_____

_____

_____

2) Our guide started forward. He stopped again. I heard it now. Out of the familiar, hollow tautophony of drumbeats there began to emerge a thread of actual melody—an untraditional rise and fall of notes—a **tentative** attack as it were, on the chromatic scale of the west. No he-goat's skin stretched on bamboo would do that. We pushed on, curious. We came out into the "place."

_____

_____

_____

3) If mail trains can carry mail, with parcels up to 7 lbs. in weight at the same price for any distance, why cannot all trains carry passengers and goods of any size and weight at the same price for any distance? The answer is that they can. It is the object of this pamphlet to prove not only that it is possible financially, but that, with the small **uniform** fares and rates indicated on the title page, sufficient revenue can be obtained to pay working expenses and provide the sum required to purchase the whole of the existing railway. Undertakings at their full market price or such a price as willing vendors would be ready to accept is possible to achieve.

_____

_____

_____

_____

4) The friends of the host all gathered around in anticipation of the one they thought would be the thrill of the night. Just five minutes prior it was announced that he arrived in the building. The five minutes seemed to draw out to five hours – all eyes were fixed on the door. Suddenly, the lights went out, and a wind could be felt in the apartment. "Hey, what are you trying to pull by turning out the lights, trying to scare us?" Behind them all, a dim light began to glow and encompass a figure who said, " Scare you? With lights? Do not take me for some **practitioner** of cheap light tricks!"

_____

_____

_____

_____

5) The philosophers, who have examined the **foundations** of society, have every one of them, perceived the necessity of tracing it back to a state of nature, but not one of them has ever arrived there. Some of them have not hesitated to attribute to man in that state the ideas of justice and injustice, without troubling their heads to prove, that he really must have had such ideas, or even that such ideas were useful to him. Others have spoken of the natural right of every man to keep what belongs to him, without letting us know what they meant by the word belong.

_____

_____

_____

_____

Unit 26-30 Review

Match the correct definition with the correct word by writing the correct definition' letter in the blank next to the word that corresponds to that definition.

____ 1. Grade   A. Powerfully effective

____ 2. Challenge   B. Capable of reasoning

____ 3. Falter   C. Consistent; conforming to one standard

____ 4. Discord   D. An expression of grief, suffering, or sadness

____ 5. Transparent   E. A donation or legacy to support a charitable institution, and constituting a permanent fund

____ 6. Foundation   F. A slope (up or down) of a roadway or other passage

____ 7. Uniform   G. To waver or be unsteady

____ 8. Rational   H. A confrontation, a dare

____ 9. Lament   I. Lack of agreement, or harmony

____ 10. Potent   J. Open for all to know, thereby reducing the chance of corruption

Fill in the blanks with the correct word from this unit's words:

From _____ cherry blossoms to a fresh sea breeze, perfumes capture pleasing fragrances for people to wear. The word "perfume" is _____ from the Latin word *perfumare*, which means "to smoke through". A _____ and effective perfume has a carefully blended balance of low, middle, and high notes, which fade in succession to make the perfume last a long time. The _____ of all perfumes is the "heart", which is made up of a few main ingredients, like essential oils and aroma compounds. These fragrances are often _____ directly from their sources, which can include flowers and other plants, woods, leathers or foods.

Answer Keys

Unit 1	Unit 2	Unit 3	Unit 4	Unit 5
B) Sentences	**B) Sentences**	**B) Sentences**	**B) Sentences**	**B) Sentences**
Def 4 advocate	Def 3 individual	Def 2 formula	Def 2 concepts	Def 4 feature
Def 1 definition	Def 1 major	Def 4 approached	Def 1 significant	Def 2 strategy
Def 1 advocate	Def 4 authority	Def 4 documented	Def 3 scruple	Def 3 resourced
Def 2 definitions	Def 2 commodities	Def 3 approached	Def 3 utilize	Def 2 acquired
Def 1 consequent	Def 1 individual	Def 1 formula	Def 3 processes	Def 1 feature
Def 4 definition	Def 3 authority	Def 3 documented	Def 2 process	Def 2 resources
Def 2 fundamental	Def 3 major	Def 2 approaching	Def 2 scruple	Def 2 feature
Def 1 industrious	Def 2 complacent	Def 3 formula	Def 1 utilize	Def 1 resources
Def 5 definition	Def 2 authority	Def 1 approached	Def 1 process	Def 6 featured
Def 2 consequent	Def 1 complacent	Def 4 formula	Def 2 utilize	Def 3 strategy
Def 6 definition	Def 5 majoring	Def 2 documents	Def 4 processed	Def 7 featured
Def 3 fundamental	Def 2 individual	Def 1 unprecedented	Def 3 significant	Def 1 strategies
Def 2 advocate	Def 2 major	Def 2 sectioned	Def 1 concept	Def 1 ensure
Def 1 fundamentals	Def 1 authority	Def 5 approach	Def 5 process	Def 5 feature
Def 3 advocated	Def 1 commodities	Def 1 document	Def 1 scrupulous	Def 2 ensure
Def 3 definition	Def 4 major	Def 1 section	Def 2 significant	Def 1 acquired
				Def 3 feature
C) Paragraphs	**C) Paragraphs**	**C) Paragraphs**	**C) Paragraphs**	**C) Paragraphs**
Def 2	Def 1	Def 2	Def 1	Def 3
Def 1	Def 1	Def 2	Def 3	Def 2
Def 2	Def 3	Def 1	Def 1	Def 1
Def 1	Def 1	Def 2	Def 1	Def 1
Def 4	Def 2	Def 1	Def 2	Def 2

Unit Review 1-5

1. Feature	B	A.	To make an attempt at as in solving a problem
2. Commodity	J	B.	To state or show that something is the greatest importance to another thing within a certain context
3. Complacent	G	C.	To plead in favor of
4. Process	E	D.	Never before seen, done, or experienced
5. Fundamental	H	E.	To think about a piece of information
6. Approach	A	F.	Something that is used to achieve an objective
7. Resource	F	G.	Not caring with regard to an apparent need or problem
8. Advocate	C	H.	Pertaining to the foundation or basis
9. Unprecedented	D	I.	Exactly and carefully done
10. Scrupulous	I	J.	An essential good from agriculture, raw materials

While it is important that elementary school teachers teach math, language arts, science, and other subjects, their primary focus should be on helping students build up **industrious** work and study habits for their future educational career. Well-**documented** research suggests that this is best done through as much one-on-one instruction with the teacher as possible. A competent teacher will know how to balance teaching an entire classroom while **ensuring** his or her students get the **individual** attention they need as well. This is a **process**; every teacher must take the time to find what works best between themselves and their students.

Focus On: Vocabulary

Unit 6	Unit 7	Unit 8	Unit 9	Unit 10
B) Sentences	B) Sentences	B) Sentences	B) Sentences	B) Sentences
Def 2 security	Def 4 interpreted	Def 2 select	Def 1 project	Def 3 constant
Def 3 taut	Def 2 circumstance	Def 5 focus	Def 5 projecting	Def 4 labeled
Def 3 role	Def 3 framework	Def 2 illustrate	Def 1 convert	Def 1 dominion
Def 1 variable	Def 2 doctrine	Def 3 selected	Def 2 substantiated	Def 2 label
Def 4 security	Def 2 eccentric	Def 4 response	Def 2 converts	Def 2 dominion
Def 2 role	Def 1 interpret	Def 2 response	Def 2 projects	Def 1 label
Def 1 security	Def 1 doctrines	Def 2 focus	Def 2 compute	Def 5 constant
Def 2 variable	Def 1 eccentric	Def 1 suffrage	Def 1 immigrated	Def 1 participated
Def 1 equate	Def 1 circumstances	Def 1 illustrate	Def 3 converted	Def 1 initial
Def 3 securities	Def 1 framework	Def 4 focus	Def 3 project	Def 3 label
Def 1 role	Def 3 eccentric	Def 1 response	Def 1 substantiate	Def 2 constant
Def 2 taut	Def 3 interprets	Def 1 focus	Def 6 Projecting	Def 3 dominion
Def 4 variables	Def 3 circumstances	Def 3 response	Def 4 converted	Def 1 constant
Def 1 taut	Def 2 framework	Def 1 select	Def 1 compute	Def 2 initial
Def 3 variable	Def 2 interpret	Def 3 focus	Def 4 projects	Def 5 labeled
			Def 5 converted	Def 4 constant
C) Paragraphs	C) Paragraphs	C) Paragraphs	C) Paragraphs	C) Paragraphs
Def 3	Def 3	Def 5	Def 5	Def 1
Def 2	Def 2	Def 1	Def 1	Def 1
Def 2	Def 3	Def 3	Def 4	Def 5
Def 1	Def 3	Def 1	Def 1	Def 1
Def 1	Def 2	Def 1	Def 1	Def 5

Unit Review 6-10

1. Taut	I	A.	Of high quality
2. Eccentric	G	B.	A name given to something or someone to categorize them as part of a particular social group.
3. Doctrine	J	C.	Marked by diversity or difference.
4. Project	H	D.	Steady in purpose, action, feeling, etc.
5. Constant	D	E.	A point at which reflected or refracted rays of light converge.
6. Variable	C	F.	A person who is now in favor of something that he or she previously opposed
7. Label	B	G.	Behaving unexpectedly or differently
8. Select	A	H.	To make plans for
9. Convert	F	I.	Containing only relevant parts
10. Focus	E	J.	A statement or belief of fundamental government

The **framework** for a good college course requires a well-structured and **focused** curriculum that covers all relevant topics for the subject. From the professor's **initial** meeting with the students, he or she must present an adequate syllabus and build rapport with the students, assuring them that he or she is organized and knowledgeable. It is important to **substantiate** this type of first impression which will establish the professor's position and encourage class participation later on in the semester. Though the personalities of the students are a **variable** out of the professor's control, the professor should do what he or she can to put his or her best foot forward and prepare the students for a great semester.

Focus On: Vocabulary

Unit 11	Unit 12	Unit 13	Unit 14	Unit 15
B) Sentences	B) Sentences	B) Sentences	B) Sentences	B) Sentences
Def 4 commit	Def 1 resolution	Def 1 research	Def 4 set	Def 2 prior
Def 1 perceive	Def 1 contrast	Def 3 negated	Def 2 enable	Def 1 symbol
Def 3 available	Def 1 dismay	Def 3 stress	Def 2 ponder	Def 2 grant
Def 5 minored	Def 3 contrasts	Def 2 coordinate	Def 1 set	Def 2 symbol
Def 2 committed	Def 3 resolution	Def 3 researching	Def 1 enable	Def 5 grant
Def 2 available	Def 1 egregious	Def 1 stresses	Def 2 set	Def 1 specify
Def 1 minor	Def 4 phases	Def 1 coordinates	Def 1 pragmatic	Def 4 grant
Def 3 committed	Def 4 resolution	Def 2 stress	Def 3 set	Def 1 prior
Def 3 Minors	Def 3 phases	Def 4 researching	Def 1 ignorance	Def 2 transit
Def 5 commit	Def 5 resolution	Def 1 negate	Def 5 sets	Def 3 prior
Def 1 dimension	Def 7 resolution	Def 2 researches	Def 1 pondering	Def 3 grant
Def 1 commit	Def 1 phase	Def 4 stress	Def 7 set	Def 4 prior
Def 2 dimensions	Def 2 phases	Def 2 negates	Def 3 enabled	Def 3 symbols
Def 2 minor	Def 2 contrasts	Def 1 predict	Def 6 set	Def 1 granted
Def 1 available	Def 6 resolution		Def 8 sets	Def 1 transit
Def 4 minor				Def 6 grant
Def 3 dimensions				
C) Paragraphs	C) Paragraphs	C) Paragraphs	C) Paragraphs	C) Paragraphs
Def 5	Def 1	Def 2	Def 2	Def 4
Def 2	Def 1	Def 1	Def 1	Def 1
Def 2	Def 1	Def 1	Def 3	Def 3
Def 1	Def 1	Def 2	Def 1	Def 2
Def 1	Def 1	Def 2	Def 1	Def 1

Units Review 11-15

1. Resolution	F	A.	A subject area of secondary concentration of a student at a college or university
2. Commit	H	B.	To think of deeply
3. Grant	E	C.	To apply force to (a body or structure) causing strain.
4. Coordinate	I	D.	To become solid
5. Prior	G	E.	The deed or writing by which such a transfer (of land or money) is made
6. Stress	C	F.	A vow
7. Phase	J	G.	Coming before
8. Minor	A	H.	To give in trust
9. Ponder	B	I.	To cause two or more events to happen at exactly the same time
10. Set	D	J.	How something appears to the eye, especially with different and varying appearances of the same object

To his **dismay**, James **perceived** that Mrs. Angelo was not fond of him for some reason. He could tell this from the harsh tone of her voice towards him, the glares she shot at him in class, and how she **negated** everything he said, even if it was a fact. She made her disdain for him quite obvious to the entire class as well. He **pondered** different ways he could try to win her favor before the school year ended, and wondered if perhaps he could write her a thank you card and gift her some chocolates as **symbols** of his appreciation to her for being his teacher. For now, all he could do was be on his best behavior and stay out of trouble.

Focus On: Vocabulary

Unit 16	Unit 17	Unit 18	Unit 19	Unit 20
B) Sentences	B) Sentences	B) Sentences	B) Sentences	B) Sentences
Def 3 dominate	Def 4 draft	Def 1 generate	Def 6 elements	Def 1 relative
Def 4 objective	Def 3 series	Def 3 constrain	Def 4 recovery	Def 2 conducted
Def 3 environment	Def 3 migrated	Def 4 abstract	Def 3 elements	Def 3 investigated
Def 1 dominate	Def 2 integrated	Def 2 generate	Def 1 recovery	Def 2 logic
Def 4 environment	Def 1 series	Def 1 asserted	Def 2 corresponding	Def 1 conducted
Def 1 undermined	Def 1 contended	Def 2 technique	Def 2 element	Def 2 investigate
Def 5 dominate	Def 2 series	Def 1 abstracts	Def 1 transform	Def 3 estates
Def 1 objective	Def 1 draft	Def 3 assert	Def 5 element	Def 4 conducted
Def 2 dominated	Def 1 migrate	Def 1 constrained	Def 2 transform	Def 2 relative
Def 1 subjective	Def 2 migrated	Def 4 generated	Def 1 correspond	Def 1 logic
Def 2 objective	Def 3 draft	Def 1 techniques	Def 3 recovery	Def 1 investigate
Def 1 environment	Def 2 contend	Def 2 asserted	Def 1 statistic	Def 3 relatives
Def 2 environment	Def 1 integrated	Def 3 abstract	Def 1 elements	Def 3 conducts
Def 4 dominates	Def 4 migrating	Def 3 generated	Def 2 statistic	Def 1 estate
Def 3 objective	Def 3 integrated	Def 2 constrained	Def 4 element	Def 5 conduct
	Def 2 draft	Def 3 technique	Def 2 recovery	Def 2 estate
	Def 4 series	Def 2 abstract		Def 3 logic
C) Paragraphs	C) Paragraphs	C) Paragraphs	C) Paragraphs	C) Paragraphs
Def 1	Def 1	Def 1	Def 1	Def 2
Def 1	Def 3	Def 2	Def 1	Def 1
Def 1	Def 2	Def 3	Def 1	Def 2
Def 2	Def 2	Def 2	Def 2	Def 1
Def 3	Def 1	Def 3	Def 1	Def 2

Units 16-20 Review

1. Objective	J	A.	The theoretical way of looking at things
2. Element	H	B.	To maintain or defend, as a cause or a claim
3. Conduct	D	C.	Renewed growth after an economic slowdown
4. Draft	I	D.	To carry out
5. Relative	G	E.	To overlook from a height
6. Recovery	C	F.	To include as a constituent part or functionality
7. Assert	B	G.	Connected to or depending on something else
8. Abstract	A	H.	A group of people within a larger group having a particular common characteristic
9. Integrate	F	I.	An order for money to be paid
10. Dominate	E	J.	Not influenced by personal feelings or opinions in considering and representing facts

Panic struck Joanne; it was her first time being the lead detective, and she hadn't the slightest clue on how to **integrate** the DNA analysis team into the police department for this case. Previous attempts had led to a hostile work **environment**, the dissolution of the combined team, and an unsolved case. Vincent, another detective, broke the silence. "Your silence shows that maybe you aren't cut out for this, Jo", he said snidely. Joanne struggled within herself. *Are you going to let him talk to you like that in front of everyone, Joanne? No way!* With piercing eye contact, her demeanor **transformed**. "There's no need to speak to me that way, Vincent. I was organizing my thoughts on how to start **generating** ideas. Now team, how shall we proceed with **investigating** this crime?"

Focus On: Vocabulary

Unit 21	Unit 22	Unit 23	Unit 24	Unit 25
B) Sentences	B) Sentences	B) Sentences	B) Sentences	B) Sentences
Def 2 fiscal	Def 1 brief	Def 2 pursue	Def 1 peculiar	Def 2 declines
Def 1 index	Def 5 yields	Def 1 presume	Def 1 complex	Def 2 option
Def 2 avenues	Def 1 sauntered	Def 2 emerged	Def 3 decreed	Def 1 allocate
Def 6 indexing	Def 2 brief	Def 2 conflict	Def 3 domain	Def 1 accurate
Def 1 subsequent	Def 1 plausible	Def 1 conflict	Def 2 peculiar	Def 5 decline
Def 5 indexes	Def 2 yield	Def 2 presumed	Def 2 decrees	Def 3 option
Def 3 reproach	Def 2 Summary	Def 1 imposes	Def 1 domain	Def 3 decline
Def 3 avenues	Def 2 plausible	Def 3 emerged	Def 2 complex	Def 2 ethnic
Def 2 index	Def 5 briefs	Def 1 pursue	Def 5 Domain	Def 2 allocated
Def 1 reproaches	Def 1 yield	Def 2 impose	Def 3 complex	Def 4 decline
Def 1 avenue	Def 3 brief	Def 1 emerged	Def 2 domain	Def 3 allocates
Def 1 fiscal	Def 3 summaries	Def 4 conflict	Def 5 complex	Def 2 accurate
Def 3 index	Def 4 yields	Def 3 pursues	Def 1 eloquent	Def 1 ethnic
Def 2 reproached	Def 4 brief	Def 3 imposes	Def 4 complexes	Def 1 options
Def 2 subsequent	Def 1 summary	Def 3 conflicted	Def 1 decree	Def 1 declined
Def 4 index	Def 3 yield		Def 4 domain	
C) Paragraphs	C) Paragraphs	C) Paragraphs	C) Paragraphs	C) Paragraphs
Def 1	Def 4	Def 3	Def 1	Def 4
Def 1	Def 3	Def 2	Def 4	Def 2
Def 1	Def 2	Def 3	Def 2	Def 1
Def 4	Def 2	Def 2	Def 1	Def 3
Def 1	Def 1	Def 2	Def 1	Def 2

Unit 21-25 Review

1. Presume	H	A.	Seemingly or apparently valid, likely, or acceptable
2. Decree	F	B.	To enforce; compel to behave in a certain way
3. Allocate	I	C.	To criticize someone
4. Domain	G	D.	To stroll, or walk at a leisurely pace
5. Fiscal	J	E.	To refuse
6. Saunter	D	F.	An edict or law
7. Plausible	A	G.	A group of related items, topics, or subjects.
8. Decline	E	H.	To assume or suggest to be true
9. Impose	B	I.	To distribute according to a plan
10. Reproach	C	J.	Pertaining to finance and money in general

Fiscal policy, more widely used after World War II, is one way the government of the United States influences the nation's economy. Fiscal policy is implemented by either a) adjusting the tax rate, or b) adjusting government spending. Monetary policy, another tool of government influence, **emerged** around the same time. These two policies are used in a mix, depending on the economic goals of the country. Influencing an entire economy, however, is a rather **complex** task, and could **yield** unfavorable results if the effects are not calculated properly. To avoid a **decline** in economic growth, economists must carefully consider what to do to stimulate the economy through fiscal policy.

Unit 26	Unit 27	Unit 28	Unit 29	Unit 30
B) Sentences	B) Sentences	B) Sentences	B) Sentences	B) Sentences
Def 3 challenge	Def 4 flourish	Def 2 rational	Def 2 demonstrated	Def 6 foundation
Def 4 potent	Def 5 grade	Def 4 extract	Def 1 adapt	Def 4 drone
Def 1 disdain	Def 1 transparent	Def 3 pinnacle	Def 1 prescribed	Def 1 tentative
Def 4 challenge	Def 2 restricted	Def 1 lamented	Def 5 falter	Def 2 uniform
Def 2 definite	Def 3 flourished	Def 1 pinnacle	Def 1 demonstrated	Def 1 foundation
Def 6 challenge	Def 1 grade	Def 2 extract	Def 3 falter	Def 2 practitioner
Def 3 definite	Def 1 discriminate	Def 2 lament	Def 2 prescribe	Def 1 drones
Def 3 potent	Def 3 grade	Def 3 rational	Def 2 discord	Def 5 foundation
Def 1 challenges	Def 1 flourishing	Def 1 extract	Def 4 falter	Def 1 uniform
Def 1 potent	Def 4 grades	Def 1 comprehensive	Def 2 adapted	Def 4 foundations
Def 1 obvious	Def 2 discriminating	Def 5 extracted	Def 3 discord	Def 2 tentative
Def 5 challenge	Def 6 grade	Def 4 pinnacles	Def 1 faltered	Def 2 drone
Def 2 potent	Def 2 flourished	Def 1 rational	Def 3 adapted	Def 2 foundations
Def 2 challenge	Def 1 restricted	Def 3 extract	Def 1 discord	Def 3 uniforms
Def 1 Definite	Def 2 grades	Def 2 pinnacle	Def 2 falter	Def 3 foundation
	Def 2 transparent			Def 1 practitioner
				Def 3 drone
C) Paragraphs	C) Paragraphs	C) Paragraphs	C) Paragraphs	C) Paragraphs
Def 5	Def 3	Def 4	Def 2	Def 4
Def 4	Def 2	Def 1	Def 4	Def 2
Def 1	Def 2	Def 2	Def 1	Def 2
Def 3	Def 1	Def 1	Def 1	Def 1
Def 1	Def 1	Def 1	Def 1	Def 2

Unit 26-30 Review

1. Grade	F	A.	Powerfully effective.	
2. Challenge	H	B.	Capable of reasoning	
3. Falter	G	C.	Consistent; conforming to one standard.	
4. Discord	I	D.	An expression of grief, suffering, or sadness.	
5. Transparent	J	E.	A donation or legacy to support a charitable institution, and constituting a permanent fund	
6. Foundation	E	F.	A slope (up or down) of a roadway or other passage	
7. Uniform	C	G.	To waver or be unsteady	
8. Rational	B	H.	A confrontation, a dare	
9. Lament	D	I.	Lack of agreement or harmony	
10. Potent	A	J.	Open for all to know, thereby reducing the chance of corruption	

From **flourishing** cherry blossoms to a fresh sea breeze, perfumes capture pleasing fragrances for people to wear. The word "perfume" is **adapted** from the Latin word *perfumare*, which means "to smoke through". A **potent** and effective perfume has a carefully blended balance of low, middle, and high notes, which fade in succession to make the perfume last a long time. The **foundation** of all perfumes is the "heart", which is made up of a few main ingredients, like essential oils and aroma compounds. These fragrances are often **extracted** directly from their sources, which can include flowers and other plants, woods, leathers or foods.

Other SAT® Books by Focus on Learning Publishing, LLC.®

Achieving the SAT® Breakthrough: Acing the Types of Questions that Most Students Find Difficult

Focus On: Line Reference Questions

Achieving the SAT® Breakthrough: Acing the Types of Questions that Most Students Find Difficult

Focus on: Big & Small Idea Questions

Achieving the SAT® Breakthrough: Acing the Types of Questions that Most Students Find Difficult

Focus On: Inference Questions

Achieving the SAT® Breakthrough: Acing the Types of Questions that Most Students Find Difficult

Focus On: Informational Graphics

E-Book – Back to the SAT® Basics: Reading Comprehension for High School Students –

Focus On: Main Idea, Details, and Summarizing with Short News Based Articles

Go to www.folpbooks.com for downloads, books, and updates

Some downloads include:

Free root words and root words' tests
Free SAT® type reading passages to get even more practice with the types of passages on the test
Free extra work on all of our books
And much more!

Made in United States
North Haven, CT
25 July 2022